Voices of the Mind

Theoretical Imagination in Psychology Series

Series Editor: Gün Semin, Professor of Social Psychology
Free University, Amsterdam

This exciting new series gives students access to and analysis of diverse intellectual traditions in psychology previously not readily available because of language, cultural, and political barriers. Each book, written by an internationally acclaimed scholar, builds a bridge between issues of central importance in psychology and the new, sometimes unknown, theoretical insights they introduce. Each focuses not only on the work of influential thinkers but also on broad intellectual traditions; and, moreover, each invites a restructuring of traditional thinking within the discipline of psychology.

Voices
of the Mind

A Sociocultural Approach to
Mediated Action

———

James V. Wertsch

HARVESTER
WHEATSHEAF

London   Sydney   Singapore

British Library Cataloguing in Publication Data
Wertsch, James V.
  Voices of the mind : a sociocultural approach to mediated
  action.
  1. Cognitive social psychology
  I. Title
  302

  ISBN 0-7450-1008-3
  ISBN 0-7450-1009-1 pbk

Published 1991 by
Harvester Wheatsheaf
66 Wood Lane End, Hemel Hempstead
Hertfordshire, HP2 4RG
A division of
Simon & Schuster International Group

Printed in the United States of America

10 9 8 7 6 5 4 3 2 1

To Mary Louise Wertsch
and to the memory of
Clifford Henry Wertsch

Preface

The aim of the Theoretical Imagination in Psychology series is to provide access to diverse intellectual traditions, both within and outside the field of psychology, which have not, for a number of reasons, been readily available before to students and teachers. Language has certainly been a barrier. Another has been the classic problem that certain intellectual developments do not fall onto fertile ground because they go against the grain of the prevailing *Zeitgeist*. And certain traditions do not find entry into the disciplinary imagination, despite their potential relevance, because they must await intellectual bridge-builders.

Such bridge-builders often issue an invitation to reconsider existing theoretical and empirical issues in a different light. This is precisely what James Wertsch does in *Voices of the Mind*. He makes a provocative theoretical and empirical contribution to psychology which provides a framework for understanding the sociocultural and historical context of human mental processes. On the one hand, he provides a synthesis between two intellectual traditions and, on the other, he develops a model of how human action is situated in cultural, historical, and institutional settings.

The traditions he draws upon originate in Vygotsky's sociocultural approach to the study of mind—namely, the idea that human activity is mediated by signs. But a close examination of Vygotsky's contribution to the social origins of higher mental functioning reveals the absence of theoretical and empirical reference to broader historical, institutional, or cultural processes. In developing a theory of *mediated action* Wertsch complements Vygotsky's perspective with Bakhtin's approach to "meaning," with special reference to social language and speech genres. He develops a model of the relationship between psychological processes and sociocultural settings and shows how mental processes are mediated by communication that is historically, culturally, and socially situated. In examining the implications of his original synthesis, Wertsch provides diverse empirical illustrations ranging from political to educational settings. In developing a synthesis of mediated action, he provides an original and stimulating approach to understanding the broader social context of human mental processes and their situated features.

There is a growing awareness in psychological circles about the culturally situated nature of mental processes. This awareness is gathering considerable momentum in such diverse fields as social psychology, personality studies, and cognitive and developmental psychology. It is becoming apparent that an understanding of human cognition and cognitive processes cannot be explored in a framework that detaches mental activities from sociocultural settings. *Voices of the Mind* is a timely investigation of the limits of these boundaries and an innovative challenge to psychological thinking.

Gün Semin
Amsterdam
November 1990

Contents

Voices of the Mind

Introduction

I n a time of unprecedented interest in psychological phenomena, it is ironic that the discipline of psychology seems less capable than ever of providing a coherent account of the human mind. We
know more about isolated mental processes and skills, but we seem
incapable of generating an overall picture of mental functioning. We
can often find regularities under controlled laboratory conditions, but
as soon as we move to other, more natural settings these findings seem
to disappear in the sea of "real life." Such problems do not stem from
an absence of resources or of effort on the part of psychologists. There
are more researchers and practitioners, more journals, more professional organizations, and more computers devoted to psychology today than ever before. Yet the results are increasingly less satisfactory
if we stand back and ask what psychology tells us about human nature.

This is not to say there are not some bright spots. We know far
more about brain functioning than we did even a few years ago, we
have a much richer picture of the social and cognitive functioning of
infants than we had earlier, and a variety of new forms of psychother-
apy seems to provide help where none existed before. I do not wish
to underplay the significance of these scientific accomplishments or the
major practical benefits associated with them. Even the brief list I have
provided, however, serves to highlight a fundamental weakness of the
discipline: we have many isolated, often arcane pieces to a larger puzzle, but we have no coherent, integrative picture of the whole. We can
answer detailed questions about neuronal activity or neonatal reflexes,
but we have very little to say about what it means to be human in the
modern world (or any other world for that matter). Jerome Bruner's

(1976) comments about the problems psychology has had in creating a coherent "image of man" are as apt today as they were fifteen years ago.

One of the most striking manifestations of this weakness is that psychology has become increasingly less capable of providing insights into the major social issues of the day. It often has something to offer if one is concerned with a specific clinical syndrome or brain dysfunction, but it has had very little impact on broader social and cultural issues such as educational failure and educational reform.

That the discipline of psychology has been silent on major social issues was made obvious during the recent revolutionary events in Eastern Europe and the Soviet Union. In trying to understand these events, ordinary citizens and professional commentators from around the world spoke of the psychological changes being experienced by entire populations, yet they did not find it useful or necessary to turn to psychologists or psychological theories for enlightenment.

Before exploring why this is so, I should note that I do not believe that an adequate account of political revolutions—or any other form of social change—can be reduced to some kind of psychological analysis. Nor do I wish to suggest that all psychologists must be concerned with political or social issues. Many other practical concerns have provided a focus for much of the best research being carried out today, and indeed, studies with a purely theoretical motivation often contribute more to our understanding of applied problems than work aimed directly at dealing with them.

What I do wish to argue, however, is that much contemporary research in psychology does not in fact have the practical implications so often claimed for it. In my view, a major reason is the tendency of psychological research, especially in the United States, to examine human mental functioning as if it exists in a cultural, institutional, and historical vacuum. Research is often based on the assumption that it is possible, even desirable, to study the individual, or specific areas of mental functioning in the individual, in isolation. In some cases its proponents justify this approach by claiming that we must simplify the problems we address if we are to get concrete research under way. Only then, it is argued, can we go on to understand how cultural, historical, or institutional "variables" enter into the picture.

Such criticism is not new. It has been raised in American psychology at least since the time of John Dewey. In his presidential address to the American Psychological Association entitled "Psychology and Social

Practice," Dewey (1901) argued that the discipline could not deal with the many phenomena it sought to examine if it continued to focus so exclusively on the individual organism. In his view, psychology would have to come to terms with how individuals are culturally, historically, and institutionally situated before it could understand many aspects of mental functioning.

As Seymour Sarason (1981) points out, however, Dewey's ideas never attained prominence, at least in American psychology. Most APA presidential addresses reflect the fact that "from its inception a hundred years ago, American psychology has been quintessentially a psychology of the individual organism" (p. 827). This individualistic orientation is characteristic of the discipline in general and certainly exists in studies of children's development, an area that will be of particular interest here. As Barbara Rogoff (1990) notes, "an emphasis on the individual has characterized decades of research carried out by American investigators studying children's intellectual milestones, IQ, memory strategies, and grammatical skills. It has also been characteristic of the incorporation of Piaget's theory into American research in the modern era" (p. 4).

One devastating effect of the tendency to study the isolated individual or mental process "in vacuo" (Rommetveit, 1979) has been to cut psychology off from dialogue with other academic disciplines and with the general public. Instead of participating in the construction of a coherent theory of the human mind and human action, debates in psychology have all too often devolved into arcane internal arguments of little interest to anyone but those directly involved. This is a sorry state of affairs for the social sciences and for academic inquiry in general, and it has been particularly unfortunate for psychology.

But the problems I am outlining are not only of an intellectual nature. They are also manifested in the institutional structure of contemporary psychology. Psychologists often argue that because their discipline has become so complicated, fragmentation is an unfortunate but inevitable fact of life. According to this view it is next to impossible to keep up with what is going on in one's particular division of the American Psychological Association, let alone in the field in general, and any attempt to keep abreast of developments in other disciplines is completely out of the question.

There is no doubt that unprecedented burdens have been placed on contemporary scholars of psychology by new technology, the explosion of research findings, and the creation of new subdisciplines. I do believe, however, that it is possible to formulate research problems so that areas of inquiry do not become cut off from one another. This involves conducting research (often of a quite specialized nature) into concrete empirical problems but in such a way that it always remains anchored in some more general picture.

It is not possible to do this simply by expending additional effort. That is, I am not suggesting that the next generation of psychologists should have an advanced degree in sociology, literature, physics, or some other discipline as well as in psychology. In fact, such a practice would probably only result in new forms of intellectual subspecialization. Rather, we need to reformulate the questions we ask so that disciplinary and subdisciplinary integration will be a natural, or even necessary, outcome. We need to develop the type of theoretical frameworks that can be understood and extended by researchers from a range of what now exist as separate disciplinary perspectives. Furthermore, and perhaps even more important, we need to formulate methodologies that do not automatically exclude the participation of researchers from a variety of disciplines.

As Vladimir Zinchenko (1985) and others have suggested, a key aspect of this process is creating units of analysis that work against the tendency toward disciplinary fragmentation and isolation. Too often, the choices we make lock us into a set of implicit commitments that may or may not be desirable when viewed from a more general perspective. The notion of "mediated action" I shall outline in subsequent chapters is an attempt to meet this challenge.

The task I am describing is by no means impossible, yet it is not a task to be carried out by a single investigator. The mass of theoretical and empirical information that underlies today's research would alone make such a model inadequate. Instead, ours must be a collective effort. Relevant examples of this kind of effort can be found in recent decades, usually in situations where scholars were motivated by practical considerations to overcome the differences in perspective that so often separate them. Members of the Frankfurt School of critical theory, for example, turned to philosophy, sociology, aesthetics, psychology, and history in their effort to understand the tragic political and cultural events that swept over Europe in this century.

Another example, one which shapes much of what I shall have to say in this volume, can be found in the work of Soviet scholars between the Revolution of 1917 and the onset of the Stalinist purges in the mid-1930s. Motivated by a desire to help construct what they saw as the first grand experiment in socialism, these scholars tried to deal with practical issues that extended across disciplinary boundaries. As a result, they combined ideas from a range of what are now considered quite separate disciplines.

One can begin to understand this mix of disciplines, and of theory and practice, by considering a typical day of one of the outstanding figures of the time, L. S. Vygotsky. Such a day might have involved participating in a seminar with the philologist N. Ya. Marr, the developmental psychologist (and later neuropsychologist) A. R. Luria, and the cinematographer Sergei Eisenstein, then conducting a clinical training session for teachers of deaf children, giving a lecture to a psychoneurology meeting about semiotics, and finally, writing about the implications of Stanislavsky's methods in drama for an account of inner speech. Vygotsky dealt with many topics in a fairly cursory fashion, but his attempts to identify a set of issues that could provide the focus for an integrated, interdisciplinary effort were quite productive. They continue to inform our view of a variety of problems today, more than a half century after his death.

The approach to mind I am proposing is intended to avoid the pitfalls of psychological research that focuses narrowly on the individual or on specific mental processes in vacuo. While this approach has, of necessity, an interdisciplinary flavor, it should be recognized that it is being proposed by someone whose main areas of competence are developmental psychology and semiotics. As a result, it goes into little detail on problems of history, social theory, and other topics that must ultimately be addressed if the approach is to evolve. It is my hope, however, that what I have to say will provide a beginning, an initial framework within which the voices of psychology and semiotics can come into productive dialogue with the voices of other disciplines.

I

—

Prerequisites

The basic goal of a sociocultural approach to mind is to create an account of human mental processes that recognizes the essential relationship between these processes and their cultural, historical, and institutional settings. Such an approach is concerned with topics that arise frequently in everyday as well as academic discussions. When we speak of the American or Japanese or Russian way of thinking, for example, or the eighteenth-century mind as opposed to the twentieth-century mind, or the type of reasoning characteristic of bureaucratic rationalism, we are dealing with forms of mental functioning that are of concern to a sociocultural approach to mind.

Although these topics obviously touch on psychological issues, the discipline of psychology, with few exceptions, has had very little to say about them. This volume is meant to help redress this problem. In particular, it seeks to introduce the perspective of developmental psychology into the discussion. As I noted in the introduction, this does not simply mean applying existing theoretical constructs; it means devising new ones. Although I shall examine only a few concrete examples of sociocultural settings in order to illustrate the usefulness of these new constructs, my hope is that these will suggest further topics for more detailed investigation.

As is the case with any theoretical approach, this one rests on certain underlying assumptions. At the most basic level, these assumptions are related to what it is one is trying to describe or explain. In this connection, it is not surprising that different approaches have quite different agendas. Many psychologists have concerned themselves with the universals of mental functioning, and this emphasis on mental processes, which are assumed to be ahistorical and universal, has dominated research in contemporary western psychology. In contrast, my focus emphasizes what is socioculturally specific. In this sense it is in accord with the "cultural psychology" outlined by John Berry (1985), Michael Cole (in press), Douglas Price-Williams (1980), and Richard Shweder (1990). As Stephen Toulmin (1980) notes, the roots of cultural psychology extend back at least as far as Wilhelm Wundt (1916). In recent years, a variety of factors (Cole, in press) have inspired renewed interest in the issues this discipline addresses. At a general level, this renewed interest is grounded in the assumption that "cultural traditions and social practices regulate, express, transform, and permute the human psyche, resulting less in psychic unity for humankind than in ethnic divergences in mind, self, and emotion" (Shweder, 1990, p. 1).

By choosing to focus on either universals or sociocultural situatedness, one makes certain essential assumptions about which phenomena are interesting and deserve attention. The existence of these assumptions and their implications are not often appreciated, however, and the result has been endless misunderstanding and bogus argument. Since there are undoubtedly universal as well as socioculturally specific aspects of human mental functioning, the choice here is not simply one between sound and misguided sets of assumptions; rather, it is a choice between two different research agendas, both of which need to be addressed and, where possible, integrated.

A second, related area in which underlying assumptions often differ is over the question of what counts as an appropriate description or explanation. Investigators often disagree on this issue even when they do agree on a universal or socioculturally specific focus. A wide range of other issues arises here, but one of the most central is that of units of analysis. As V. P. Zinchenko (1985) has noted, the major schools of psychology have differed widely in their choice of such units. Behaviorists have selected stimulus-response associations, Gestalt psychologists have focused on gestalts, and Piagetians have examined schemata. Certainly, these choices are not random, but one is hard-pressed to give a definitive explanation of why one unit of analysis is inherently appropriate while others are not.

I shall try to clarify my views on what needs to be described and explained and what constitutes the appropriate method for doing so by outlining several of the assumptions inherent in the title of this volume. These assumptions involve action, the notion of voice and other forms of semiotic mediation, an approach to mental action that emphasizes diversity rather than uniformity in the processes involved, and a concern with the cultural, institutional, and historical situatedness of mediated action.

Why Action?

A fundamental assumption of a sociocultural approach to mind is that what is to be described and explained is human *action*. Furthermore, the units of analysis that will guide my line of reasoning will be grounded in action. The notion of action I have in mind owes a great deal to the various "theories of activity" that have been outlined in Soviet psychology (Leont'ev, 1959, 1975, 1981; Rubinshtein, 1957), but the influence of several other theorists will also be evident.

When action is given analytic priority, human beings are viewed as coming into contact with, and creating, their surroundings as well as themselves through the actions in which they engage. Thus action, rather than human beings or the environment considered in isolation, provides the entry point into the analysis. This contrasts on the one hand with approaches that treat the individual primarily as a passive recipient of information from the environment, and on the other with approaches that focus on the individual and treat the environment as secondary, serving merely as a device to trigger certain developmental processes.

These two views are often seen as originating with Locke (1852) and with Descartes (1908), respectively, but they continue to exert a powerful, though often unrecognized influence on contemporary psychological theories. Behaviorist and neobehaviorist theories remain grounded in assumptions similar to Locke's claims that human knowledge emerges through the impact of the environment, while contemporary theorists such as Noam Chomsky (1966) pursue an avowedly Cartesian line of reasoning. This latter perspective views the human mind largely in terms of universal, innate categories and structures, and the environment primarily in terms of how it provides material for testing innately given hypotheses and influencing developmental processes.

A basic orientation toward action is nothing new in philosophy or psychology. It was a fundamental aspect of the writings of the American Pragmatists (Mead, 1934). In addition, Jean Piaget's powerful influence has insured that the concept of action, or subject-object inter-

action, has come to be appreciated by those interested in genetic episte-
mology and developmental psychology. Recent developments in disciplines such as cognitive science reflect a similar orientation, as the
prominent role given to schemas, or patterns of action, in these disciplines attests. All these traditions are based on the assumption that, in
trying to understand mental functioning, one cannot begin with the
environment or the individual human agent in isolation. They take
action and interaction as basic analytic categories and view accounts
of the environment and human mental functioning as emerging from
them.

To say that an approach accepts some notion of action as its starting
point, however, still leaves out a great deal. Many types of action can
be distinguished, and it thus becomes essential to specify the type or
types one has in mind. A useful overview can be found in Jurgen
Habermas's (1984) account of sociological approaches. Habermas has
generated a set of categories of action that are based on the relationship
between the actor and the environment. His account of the types of
environment (or "worlds") that are relevant to such an exercise derives
from Karl Popper's "three-world" theory. In Popper's (1972) view,
"we may distinguish the following three worlds or universes: first the
world of physical objects or physical states; secondly, the world of
states of consciousness, or mental states, or perhaps behavioral dispositions to act; and thirdly, the world of *objective contents of thought*,
especially of scientific and poetic thoughts and of works of art"
(p. 106).

Following I. C. Jarvie's (1972) action-theoretic translation of Popper's three-world theory, Habermas has arrived at a general typology
of approaches to action. In considering the relation between the actor
and the first world of physical objects or physical states, Habermas
(1984) notes that "since Aristotle the concept of *teleological action* has
been at the center of the philosophical theory of action. The actor
attains an end or brings about the occurrence of a desired state by
choosing means that have promise of being successful in the given
situation and applying them in a suitable manner. The central concept
is that of a *decision* among alternative courses of action, with a view
to the realization of an end, guided by maxims, and based on an
interpretation of the situation" (p. 85). Habermas goes on to remark
that decision-theoretic and game-theoretic approaches in social sciences such as economics, sociology, and social psychology can be understood as the extension of teleological models of action to "strategic

models." In strategic models "there can enter into the agent's calculation of success the anticipation of decisions on the part of at least one additional goal-directed actor" (p. 85). In arguing that strategic models are extensions of teleological models, Habermas recognizes that "strategically acting subjects must be cognitively so equipped that for them not only physical objects but decision-making systems can appear in the world. They must expand their conceptual apparatus" (p. 88). He stresses, however, that this does not entail any difference in ontological presuppositions; instead, both types of models presuppose "*one* world, namely the objective world" (p. 87).

In teleological and strategic models of action, the relationship between actor and world is judged in terms of truth and efficacy. The goal-directed actor can "make assertions that are *true* or *false* and carry out goal-directed interventions that succeed or fail, that *achieve* or *fail to achieve* the intended effect in the world" (Habermas, 1984, p. 87). Furthermore, teleological and strategic models of action generally assume that the appropriate focus of analysis is the solitary actor entering into interaction with the objective world.

A second concept of action outlined by Habermas focuses on the relationship between the actor and Popper's second world ("states of consciousness, or mental states, or perhaps . . . behavioral dispositions"). This is the concept of "dramaturgical action," which is grounded primarily in Erving Goffman's (1959) notion of the "dramaturgical metaphor." In this type of action, "the actor evokes in his public a certain image, and impression of himself, by more or less purposefully disclosing his subjectivity. Each agent can monitor public access to the system of his own intentions, thoughts, attitudes, desires, feelings, and the like, to which only he has privileged access . . . Thus the central concept of *presentation of self* does not signify spontaneous expressive behavior but stylizing the expression of one's own experience with a view to the audience" (1984, p. 86).

As Habermas notes, there are important connections between dramaturgical action and teleological action. An actor typically carries out what Goffman terms "impression management" with strategic goals in mind. In contrast to teleological action, however, where cognition, belief, and intention play a fundamental role, in dramaturgical action "desires and feelings have a paradigmatic status" (p. 91). Furthermore, in contrast to judgments based on truth or efficacy, judgment in dramaturgical action is based on concepts of sincerity or truth*fulness* and authenticity.

For Habermas the action-theoretic translation of Popper's third world ("the world of objective contents of thought") produces "normatively regulated action." As he notes, this concept of action "does not refer to the behavior of basically solitary actors who come upon other actors in their environment, but to members of a social group who orient their action to common values . . . The individual actor complies with (or violates) a norm when in a given situation the conditions are present to which the norm has application. Norms express an agreement that obtains in a social group. All members of a group for whom a given norm has validity may expect of one another that in certain situations they will carry out (or abstain from) the actions commanded (or proscribed). The central concept of *complying with a norm* means fulfilling a generalized expectation of behavior" (p. 85).

As Habermas also notes, the normative concept of action has given rise to the role theory that occupies such an important place in sociology. The central criterion for judging an action according to the normative concept of action is neither truth nor efficacy on the one hand nor sincerity, truthfulness, or authenticity on the other. Instead, judgment is concerned with the issue of complying with a norm, something that in turn "does not have the cognitive sense of expecting a predicted event, but the normative sense that members are *entitled* to expect a certain behavior" (p. 85).

Although Habermas draws extensively on accounts of all three types of action, he has found it necessary to propose a fourth type, namely, "communicative action." "The concept of *communicative action* refers to the interaction of at least two subjects capable of speech and action who establish interpersonal relations (whether by verbal or by extraverbal means). The actors seek to reach an understanding about the action situation and their plans of action in order to coordinate their actions by way of agreement. The central concept of *interpretation* refers in the first instance to negotiating definitions of the situation which admit of consensus" (p. 86). In contrast to the first three types of action, each of which is oriented primarily to one of the three worlds proposed by Popper, communicative action is simultaneously oriented to all three. Furthermore, in contrast to the criteria used to judge each of the first three types of action, communicative action is judged according to the criterion of reaching understanding.

My comments on Habermas's analysis of types of social action hardly do justice to the set of complex issues he addresses. Yet even in this very brief overview it is clear that different accounts of action arise from quite different sets of assumptions about what is to be described and explained. In addition, these assumptions are tied to particular ideas about what analytic techniques and units are appropriate. An obvious lesson is that failure to explicate presuppositions about the type or types of action involved is likely to give rise to fundamental misunderstandings, both about what is to be explained and how it is to be explained.

Why Mediated Action?

The sociocultural approach I shall propose is concerned with a form of action that has several connections to what Habermas terms teleological action. Following in the tradition of the theory of activity proposed by A. N. Leont'ev (1975, 1981), this kind of action is goal-directed; hence, the concern with teleology. In contrast to Habermas's account of teleological action, however, this approach does not assume that the appropriate focus of analysis is the solitary actor or that there is a neat separation between ends and means.

This last point is particularly important in trying to understand the modifier *mediated* in the title. The most central claim I wish to pursue is that human action typically employs "mediational means" such as tools and language, and that these mediational means shape the action in essential ways. According to this view, it is possible, as well as useful, to make an analytic distinction between action and mediational means, but the relationship between action and mediational means is so fundamental that it is more appropriate, when referring to the agent involved, to speak of "individual(s)-acting-with-mediational-means" than to speak simply of "individual(s)." Thus, the answer to the question of who is carrying out the action will invariably identify the individual(s) in the concrete situation *and* the mediational means employed.

Why Voice?

The term *voice* is derived from the work of Soviet literary scholar, semiotician, and philosopher Mikhail Bakhtin (1981, 1984, 1986) and refers to more than an auditory signal. For Bakhtin, voice involves the much more general phenomenon of "the speaking personality, the speaking consciousness" (Holquist and Emerson, 1981). My use of this notion reflects three basic ideas shared by both Vygotsky and Bakhtin. First, it reflects the assertion that to understand human mental action one must understand the semiotic devices used to mediate such action (Wertsch, 1985c). Second, it reflects the assumption that certain aspects of human mental functioning are fundamentally tied to communicative processes. The use of the term *voice* provides a constant reminder that even psychological processes carried out by an individual in isolation are viewed as involving processes of a communicative nature.

A third, related assumption is that one can adequately understand human mental functioning only through some sort of genetic or developmental analysis. In this connection both Vygotsky and Bakhtin believed that human communicative practices give rise to mental functioning in the individual. Like the American Pragmatist George Herbert Mead (1934), who was formulating his ideas at about the same time, they were convinced that "the social dimension of consciousness is primary in time and in fact. The individual dimension of consciousness is derivative and secondary" (Vygotsky, 1979, p. 30). In this context, then, the term *voice* serves as a constant reminder that mental functioning in the individual originates in social, communicative processes.

I could, in many instances, have used the notion of *role* associated with Habermas's category of dramaturgical action in place of voice. After all, the speaking personality involves someone who takes a certain perspective or belongs to particular cultural and social categories. Yet I have chosen not to use this term for several reasons. As Habermas has noted, the notion of role is tied to a specific set of assumptions about the nature of human action. Since this analytic approach to action differs from the one that is my primary concern here, I have thought it wise not to mix the two. Furthermore, the notion of mediated action rests on assumptions about the close relationship between social communicative processes and individual psychological processes, and, as I have already noted, the notion of voice helps keep this focus in view. Finally, in accordance with Bakhtin's ideas, I shall argue that human communicative and psychological processes are characterized by a dialogicality of voices: when a speaker produces an utterance, at least two voices can be heard simultaneously. The notion of role does not adequately address such dialogicality, or multivoicedness.

Why Voices?

I have chosen to speak of *voices* rather than voice because I believe that there are multiple ways of representing reality in approaching a problem. The Bakhtinian focus on dialogicality presupposes more than one voice. In addition, the notion of "heterogeneity" in thinking (Tulviste, 1986, 1987, 1988) contrasts with the assumption, often implicit and often ethnocentric, that there is only one way, or that there is an obvious, best way, to represent the events and objects in a situation. The notion of heterogeneity calls on us to consider why certain forms of speaking and thinking (voices) rather than others are invoked on particular occasions. It also forces us to recognize that we cannot answer this question simply on the basis of the metaphor of possession, which focuses on what humans "have" in the way of concepts and skills. Instead, we must consider how and why a particular voice occupies center stage, that is, why it is "privileged" (Wertsch, 1987) in a particular setting.

Why Mind?

My use of the term *mind* rather than *cognition,* which is currently more fashionable in many psychological circles, reflects a desire to integrate a wide range of psychological phenomena. Like Vygotsky and Bakhtin, I believe that it is often difficult if not meaningless to isolate various aspects of mental processes for separate analysis. Indeed, much of what I shall have to say concerns issues that are usually considered under the heading of cognition and cognitive development. It is my hope, however, that the discussion will have relevance for those interested in other aspects of human mental life, such as self and emotion.

An account of mind and mediated action able to meet these requirements obviously cannot be tied to the individual acting in vacuo. Instead, to borrow from theorists such as Gregory Bateson (1972) and Clifford Geertz (1973), mind is viewed here as something that "extends beyond the skin" in at least two senses: it is often socially distributed and it is connected to the notion of mediation. According to the first, the terms *mind* and *mental action* can appropriately be predicated of dyads and larger groups as well as of individuals. This is not to harken back to notions of collective consciousness that have been discounted in social psychology; rather, it is to recognize the power of the insight of Vygotsky (1978, 1987), Bruner (1986), Hutchins (in press), LCHC (1983), and others that mental activities such as memory or reasoning can be socially distributed.

According to the second, mental functioning is viewed as being shaped or even defined by the mediational means it employs to carry out a task. To use a contemporary example, let us consider the case of an engineer who employs computer imaging to formulate options in designing the body of an automobile and to decide among them. Does it make sense to isolate the mental action of the individual from the mechanism that mediates this action? Indeed, is it possible to say that such action is independent of the mediational means? Probably not. This is not to say that there is not an individual moment of mental action: in the end, my interest here is in psychological processes in individuals as they carry out such action. But even if one wants to provide an account of these processes, one must ultimately invoke facts about what forms of mediation (computer hardware and software, for example) are involved.

Much of what I shall have to say concerns these two extensions of mind, so I shall not go into further detail now. My main reason for raising the issue is to point out that the notion of mind embodied in the title may not be the one some people think of when they hear the term. Rather than something that is appropriately predicated only of the individual, or even of the brain, mind is defined here in terms of its inherently social and mediational properties. Thus, even when mental action is carried out by individuals in isolation, it is inherently social in certain respects and it is almost always carried out with the help of tools such as computers, language, or number systems.

Using this understanding of mind, I hope to find a way to connect psychological processes to sociocultural setting. The units of analysis and the methods employed in many psychological theories make this very difficult. In most cases, the constraints involved certainly do not preclude consideration of any such issues—there is nothing inherent in Piaget's general formulation of schemas and the assimilation and accommodation they undergo, for example, that makes it impossible to consider sociocultural setting—yet the fact that Piaget grounded the schema in the individual's interaction with physical reality has tended to lead Piagetians to focus on certain logico-mathematical structures and processes (for example, reversibility) and to ignore issues that are not easily represented in the categories used to describe them.

Why Sociocultural?

I use the term *sociocultural* because I want to understand how mental action is situated in cultural, historical, and institutional settings. I have chosen this term rather than others (such as *cultural* or *sociohistorical*) in order to recognize the important contributions of several disciplines and schools of thought to the study of mediated action. On the one hand, I wish to recognize the contributions made by Vygotsky and his colleagues (although they typically used the term *sociohistorical* rather than *sociocultural*). On the other, I wish to recognize the contributions made by many contemporary scholars of culture (although most of the scholars I have in mind do not use the term *historical* in descriptions of what they do). In a sense, a term such as *socio-historical-cultural* would be more accurate, but it is obviously much too cumbersome.

The danger in using *sociocultural* is that the historical dimension may get short shrift. As will become evident, this is clearly not what Vygotsky had in mind. In my view, however, failing to incorporate *cultural* into the title risks an even greater error, that of reducing cultural differences to historical differences, which is precisely what Vygotsky tended to do. Building on the ideas of Hegel, Marx, Lévy-Bruhl, and others, he tended to see what we would now term cross-cultural differences as "cross-historical" differences. As Lucy and Wertsch (1987) have noted, this is a major point that distinguishes Vygotsky's ideas from those developed in American anthropology by Franz Boas, Edward Sapir, and Benjamin Lee Whorf.

The difference in views I am outlining here is not simply of interest to historians of the social sciences. As Cole and Scribner (1974) and others have argued, cultural differences, especially those between Western and developing societies, continue to be widely interpreted in psychology as differences in stages of historical development. Such claims are usually no longer explicitly stated, but the fact that implicit comparisons between the reasoning processes of children in Western societies and those of adults in "primitive" societies are still being made reflects the continuing presence of this assumption.

Vygotsky and Bakhtin

The approach I am proposing is indebted to the efforts of many theorists, but I have already mentioned the two that are of particular importance: L. S. Vygotsky (1896–1934) and M. M. Bakhtin (1895–1975). Both lived in the Soviet Union all their lives. Although they were contemporaries, it seems that they were not personally acquainted (Clark and Holquist, 1984). Leonid Radzikhovskii (1982) has argued that Vygotsky read Bakhtin's writings, but there is little in the way of obvious direct influence. Partly because they lived and worked in the same general intellectual milieu, however, their ideas are quite compatible on several counts, which has allowed me to incorporate aspects of the thinking of both into a theoretical framework that extends beyond either writer's particular set of concerns.

My basic strategy will be to examine a general sociocultural approach to mind through Vygotsky's writings and then to incorporate some of Bakhtin's ideas, in particular, *utterance, voice, social language,* and *dialogue,* to extend Vygotsky's claims about the mediation of human activity by signs.

2

A Sociocultural Approach to Mind

A sociocultural approach to mind begins with the assumption that action is mediated and that it cannot be separated from the milieu in which it is carried out. Most of the extant studies that fall under this heading involve some kind of explicit comparison between historical epochs, institutional settings, or cultural contexts. Indeed, comparative methods have provided the major tools in sociocultural research: Many studies by psychological anthropologists, for example, have involved a comparison between people in traditional and modern societies. But a sociocultural approach to mediated action need not involve explicit comparison; the main criterion is that the analysis be linked in some way with specific cultural, historical, or institutional factors. And even in the case of sociocultural studies that involve no explicit comparison, the comparative method lurks just beneath the surface, since the notion of *situatedness* implies a contrast with other possibilities.

This focus on the sociocultural situatedness of mediated action does not mean that there is no room for universals: I believe that universals exist and that they will play an important role. It stems from a belief that the universalism that has come to dominate so much of contemporary psychology makes it extremely difficult to deal in a serious, theoretically motivated way with human action in context.

In many instances, the difference between universalistic and sociocultural approaches to mind is not one of out-and-out contradiction. Rather each focuses on such different phenomena and theoretical constructs that representatives of the two find it difficult to talk to one another and often view each other's claims as irrelevant or uninteresting. Thus, universalistic approaches do not overtly preclude an analysis of sociocultural situatedness, but they tend to be formulated in a way that makes such situatedness seem trivial. Piaget's ideas about universal processes of adaptation—assimilation and accommodation—and the schemata they produce do not prevent researchers from investigating socioculturally situated development, but they have in fact tended to result in the attitude that, compared to understanding underlying, universal processes, examining sociocultural situatedness is of secondary importance. Similar tendencies have arisen in other developmental analyses.

Three Basic Themes in a Vygotskian Sociocultural Approach to Mediated Action

The sociocultural approach to mind I shall outline here takes its basic framework from the writings of L. S. Vygotsky (1929, 1934a, 1934b, 1956, 1960, 1972, 1977, 1978, 1979, 1981a, 1981b, 1981c, 1982a, 1982b, 1983a, 1983b, 1984a, 1984b, 1987). Vygotsky's approach to mental functioning was intended to address issues of sociocultural situatedness; however, he did not deal in any concrete way with many of the major topics implied by a complete approach of this kind. In some cases also, his ideas need to be amended in order to reach the goals he seemed to have in mind (Wertsch, 1985c).

Three basic themes run through Vygotsky's writings: 1) a reliance on genetic, or developmental, analysis; 2) the claim that higher mental functioning in the individual derives from social life; and 3) the claim that human action, on both the social and individual planes, is mediated by tools and signs. These themes are closely intertwined in Vygotsky's work, and much of their power derives from the ways in which they presuppose one another. It is thus somewhat artificial to isolate them, but I shall do so, at least in the beginning, for the sake of clarity.

Genetic Analysis

Genetic analysis in Vygotsky's approach is motivated by the assumption that it is possible to understand many aspects of mental functioning only if one understands their origin and the transitions they have undergone. Like theorists such as Piaget and Heinz Werner, Vygotsky made genetic analysis the very foundation of the study of mind: "To encompass in research the process of a given thing's development in all its phases and changes—from birth to death—fundamentally means to discover its nature, its essence, for 'it is only in movement that a body shows what it is.' Thus, the historical [that is, in the broadest sense of "history"] study of behavior is not an auxiliary aspect of theoretical study, but rather forms its very base" (1978, pp. 64–65). In his view, attempts to understand the nature of mental processes by analyzing only the static products of development will often be misleading. Instead of correctly identifying that various aspects of these processes emerge from the genetic transformation they have undergone, these attempts may be misled by the appearance of "fossilized" forms of behavior (Vygotsky, 1978) and will struggle (often unsuccessfully) to provide a "phenotypic" account of phenomena that can be properly understood only through "genotypic" analysis.

Genetic Domains   Partly because of the practical tasks confronting him (Wertsch and Youniss, 1987), Vygotsky focused most of his empirical research on the development of the individual (that is, on ontogenesis), in particular, the individual during childhood. But his analysis applies to several other "genetic domains" as well, specifically, phylogenesis, sociocultural history, and "microgenesis" (Wertsch, 1985c). He believed that each of these domains is governed by a unique set of explanatory principles and that what would ultimately be required is an account specifying how the genetic forces in these domains are interrelated.

Vygotsky's approach to phylogenesis rests heavily on the writings of other theorists, especially Darwin and Engels, whose influence is particularly evident in his basic acceptance of Darwinian principles of evolution and in his overriding concern with the transition from apes to humans. The main psychological phenomenon for him in this genetic domain was problem solving, and he drew on Köhler's (1921a, 1921b, 1925) ideas about tool-mediated practical action in chimpanzees and gorillas to develop some specifics about how this action compares with that in humans. In particular, he was interested in the claim that such problem-solving actions in apes are constrained by concrete contextual factors; apes remain "slaves of the situation," whereas humans have the representational means to overcome such limitations.

This focus on representational tools—a category of mediational means—reflects the basic difference between elementary and higher mental functioning that plays a central role in Vygotsky's writings in general and in his distinction between phylogenetic epochs in particular. Yet this distinction has been criticized as being unclear (Van der Veer and van Ijzendoorn, 1985), and indeed, it is in need of further elaboration. It did, however, play an essential role in the analytic framework Vygotsky developed (Wertsch, 1985c), and some version (undoubtedly one more sophisticated than that he proposed) is necessary in a sociocultural approach that seeks to understand the relationship between the biological processes of change on the one hand and historical, cultural, and institutional factors on the other.

A defining property of higher mental functioning, one which is unique to humans, is the fact that it is mediated by tools and by sign systems such as natural language. Vygotsky viewed tool use in apes as a necessary, but not sufficient, condition for the emergence of higher mental functioning. That is, a complete genetic analysis would recognize tool-mediated action as a precursor to subsequent forms of mental functioning. The principles that govern later forms of mental functioning cannot be reduced to those that apply to tool-mediated action, but neither can they be fully understood without taking into account the groundwork laid by the evolutionary phase in which tools provided the primary mediational means. This line of argument allowed Vygotsky to recognize the phylogenetic affinity between apes and humans while insisting on the qualitative gulf that separates them.

As was the case with the phylogenetic domain, Vygotsky's concern with sociocultural history was motivated in part by Marxist writings, primarily those of Marx himself (Lee, 1985). Vygotsky wished to extend Marx's ideas, which focus on political economy, in order to deal with phenomena more specifically psychological in nature. That is, he wished to address the major "methodological" problem (Zinchenko and Smirnov, 1983) that traditionally confronted Soviet psychologists: how to translate Marxist ideas into concrete psychological theory. Vygotsky's thinking about the genetic domain of sociocultural history also reflects the influence of other theorists of the time, for example, Lucien Lévy-Bruhl (1910, 1923), who were concerned with what distinguishes the mental functioning of "primitives" from that of people in modern societies. Indeed, his interest in sociocultural history played such a central role in his approach (Scribner, 1985) that in the USSR it is often labeled "sociohistorical" or "cultural-historical" (Smirnov, 1975).

Whereas Vygotsky used the distinction between elementary and higher mental functioning to deal with phylogenetic transition, he introduced a further distinction within higher (uniquely human) mental functioning to deal with genetic transitions in sociocultural history. Specifically, he developed the distinction between "rudimentary" and "advanced" higher mental functioning (Wertsch, 1985c). Although he claimed that this distinction is played out in many ways, he examined it only in terms of the abstraction and "decontextualization" (Wertsch, 1985c) of the semiotic means that mediate communication and thinking. The process of abstraction has been examined in most detail in connection with the emergence of schooled literacy. Investigators such as Luria (1976a), Scribner and Cole (1981), and Tulviste (1988) have looked at this phenomenon in a variety of ways. One of the major unresolved issues for a sociocultural approach to mind is how, other than through the influence of decontextualization associated with literacy and "literacy practice" (Scribner and Cole, 1981), mental functioning changes.

According to Vygotsky, transitions in sociocultural history are governed by a set of forces unique to this genetic domain. The principles of Darwinian evolution cannot be invoked to account for these transitions, a point reflected in A. A. Leont'ev's assertion that "such laws of evolution as, for example, the law of natural selection become invalid inside the human society" (1970, p. 124). Cole (in press) has proposed that a form of Lamarckian, as opposed to Darwinian, principles apply in the genetic domain of sociocultural history.

In Vygotsky's account, the main distinguishing feature of ontogenesis—as compared with phylogenesis and sociocultural history—is that, in the former, multiple forces of development are in operation simultaneously. Specifically, he argued (Vygotsky, 1960) that in ontogenesis, a "natural" and a "cultural," or "social," line of development interact to create the dynamics of change.

> The cultural development of the child is characterized first by the fact that it transpires under conditions of dynamic organic changes. Cultural development is superimposed on the processes of growth, maturation, and the organic development of the child. It forms a single whole with these processes. It is only through abstraction that we can separate one set of processes from others.
>
> The growth of the normal child into civilization usually involves a fusion with the processes of organic maturation. Both planes of development—the natural and the cultural—coincide and mingle with one another. The two lines of change interpenetrate one another and essentially form a single line of sociobiological formation of the child's personality. (p. 47)

As I have argued elsewhere (Wertsch, 1985c), Vygotsky did not provide a detailed definition of these two lines of development; in particular, he was unclear about the natural line. Furthermore, his claim that these two lines of development operate in isolation during early phases of ontogenesis is open to question, given recent research on infancy (Trevarthen, 1979; Uzgiris, 1989).

Yet some version of the dynamic Vygotsky envisioned between the natural and cultural lines of development in ontogenesis is still a clear desideratum for developmental psychology and one that has not been adequately met to date. Among other functions, this dynamic allowed Vygotsky to distinguish between the processes involved in ontogenesis and those involved in other genetic domains. For example, he rejected the notion that ontogenesis recapitulates sociocultural history because social forces function in relative isolation in the latter. As formulated by a member of the Vygotskian school, "in contrast to ontogenesis, the natural maturation of the brain does not play a role in the course of historical development. The natural course of the development of cognitive processes is the historical development of society" (Tulviste, 1978, p. 83).

With regard to microgenesis, Vygotsky actually dealt with two types of development. First, at several points in his writings he considered the emergence of a mental process that occurs during a single training session. He was concerned, for example, with the kind of training involved in preparing subjects for their participation in an experiment. When investigators discard data from the procedure of "training to criterion," they often discard the very data that, in his view, have the most explanatory power. A second form of microgenesis that concerned Vygotsky is the unfolding of a single psychological act (for instance, an act of perception), often over the course of milliseconds. Under this heading he examined the processes involved in the transition from thought to speech (see Vygotsky, 1987, Chapter 7).

Relationships among Genetic Domains   Whenever an approach deals with multiple genetic domains, it makes certain implicit or explicit assumptions about how the various forms of development are related. The biologist Ernst Haeckel (1874) proposed the "law of recapitulation," which asserts that the development of the individual parallels or recapitulates the development of the species. Psychologists such as G. S. Hall (1906) have similarly argued that the mental development of the individual recapitulates sociocultural history. Modern versions of this form of recapitulationism can be found in Piaget (1923) and Habermas (1984). In general, when they are explicitly formulated, most recapitulationist notions are now largely rejected in psychology; nonetheless, their implicit presence is often apparent in the methods used to collect and analyze empirical data.

Another formulation of the relationship among various genetic domains involves what Werner (1948) termed "the principle of parallelism." This approach explicitly rejects recapitulationism, recognizing the qualitative differences that distinguish, say, the thought of children in modern societies and that of adults in traditional societies. It does assert, however, that "development in mental life follows certain general and formal rules whether it concerns the individual or the species" (p. 26). The general and formal rules Werner had in mind concerned processes such as syncretism and diffusion, which characterize more primitive forms of mental functioning, as opposed to differentiation and hierarchicalization, which characterize more advanced forms. Because of the functioning of these general genetic processes, certain parallelisms may be found between ontogenesis and, say, phylogenesis. But Werner insisted that this is only a formal parallelism and that "apart from general and formal similarities, there do exist specific material differences in the comparable phenomena" (p. 26).

Vygotsky produced yet a third formulation of the relationship between the various genetic domains. In his view, each domain is governed by a unique set of principles, which precludes any form of recapitulationism and also emphasizes differences rather than similarities among domains. Like Werner, however, he did recognize some general, formal similarities among genetic domains in the type of developmental transitions involved. These similarities are grounded in Vygotsky's analysis of mediational means, an issue to which I shall return in more detail. The differences among genetic domains stem from the kinds of developmental forces involved in each.

In the case of phylogenesis, Vygotsky and Luria (1930) argued that organic evolution culminates in the use and invention of tools in humanlike apes, which in their view provided the necessary, but not sufficient, conditions for the emergence of sociocultural history. Such an interpretation is subject to the criticisms Geertz (1973) and Chris Sinha (1989) have made of "critical point" theories and must be revised accordingly (Wertsch, 1985c), but the qualitative, nonrecapitulationist relationship it sees between phylogenesis and sociocultural history is still an important and generally accepted point. According to the argument advanced by Vygotsky and Luria, once the necessary but not sufficient conditions exist, the emergence of "labor and the associated development of human speech and other psychological signs" make the transitions of sociocultural history possible (1930, p. 3). Now the site of genesis is in mediational means rather than in the gene pool.

In the case of ontogenesis, Vygotsky argued that a "cultural line of development" involving mastery of the mediational means provided by a culture is combined with a "natural line of development" involving development and maturation. The interaction of these two lines of development distinguishes this genetic domain from the others. The fact that Vygotsky said relatively little about the latter is a weakness in his analyses of ontogenetic transitions (Wertsch, 1985c). At the same time, he did conduct several insightful studies of how children master mediational means, especially language, in the cultural line of development, and these provide the impetus for much of what I shall say here.

Vygotsky's analyses of the principles that apply to the various genetic domains were often formulated in terms of his claim that "the very nature of development changes." He identified major transition points between genetic domains in terms of this "development of development." For example, in the introduction to their monograph, *Essays on the Development of Behavior: Ape, Primitive, Child,* Vygotsky and Luria (1930) characterized phylogenesis, sociocultural history, and ontogenesis in the following terms: "All three of these moments are symptoms of new epochs in the evolution of behavior and indications of *a change in the type of development itself.* In all three instances we have thereby selected turning points or critical steps in the development of behavior. We think that the turning point or critical moment in the behavior of apes is the use of tools; in the behavior of primitives it is labor and the use of psychological signs; in the behavior of the child it is the bifurcation of lines of development into natural-psychological and cultural-psychological development" (p. 4).

Social Origins of Mental Functioning in the Individual

As in other areas of his thought, Vygotsky's claim that higher mental functioning in the individual is rooted in social life was influenced by Marxist theory. At issue here is the more general claim that in order to understand the individual it is necessary to understand the social relations in which the individual exists. Marx's (1959) most succinct formulation of this idea can be found in his "Sixth Thesis on Feuerbach," which surfaces in Vygotsky's writings in the assertion that "humans' psychological nature represents the aggregate of internalized social relations that have become functions for the individual and form the individual's structure" (1981b, p. 164).

The task for Vygotsky and other theorists who have tried to translate this Marxian statement into concrete psychological terms (Seve, 1978) has been to specify the social and individual processes involved. In carrying out this task, Vygotsky followed his normal practice (Wertsch, 1985b) of integrating Marxian ideas with the ideas of other social scientists. He borrowed from the French psychiatrist and psychologist Pierre Janet (1926–27, 1928) in order to formulate his most general statement about the social origins of individual mental functioning, the "general genetic law of cultural development."

> Any function in the child's cultural development appears twice, or on two planes. First it appears on the social plane, and then on the psychological plane. First it appears between people as an interpsychological category, and then within the child as an intrapsychological category. This is equally true with regard to voluntary attention, logical memory, the formation of concepts, and the development of volition . . . [I]t goes without saying that internalization transforms the process itself and changes its structure and functions. Social relations or relations among people genetically underlie all higher functions and their relationships. (1981b, p. 163)

As its very name makes clear, in addition to dealing with the second theme that runs throughout Vygotsky's writings, the general genetic law of cultural development is also closely tied to his first theme, genetic analysis. According to this view, an examination of the precursors to *intramental** functioning (that is, of *intermental* functioning) is the key to understanding mental functioning in the individual.

The general genetic law of cultural development entails several claims that are neither widely shared nor even understood in contemporary psychology. The first involves much more than the idea that

---

*Following the practice of Minick (Vygotsky, 1987), I shall employ the terms "intermental" and "intramental" as translations of *interpsikhicheskii* and *intrapsikhicheskii*, respectively. This is more consistent with other translations of the term *psikhicheskii* as "mental" in Wertsch (1981) and Vygotsky (1978), where the terms "interpsychological" (vs. "intermental") and "intrapsychological" (vs. "intramental") were used.

mental functioning in the individual derives from participation in social life; it argues that the specific structures and processes of intramental functioning can be traced to their genetic precursors on the intermental plane. In Vygotsky's words, "[higher mental functions'] composition, genetic structure, and means of action [forms of mediation]—in a word, their whole nature—is social. Even when we turn to mental [internal] processes, their nature remains quasi-social. In their own private sphere, human beings retain the functions of social interaction" (1981b, p. 164). Vygotsky does not assume that higher mental functioning in the individual is a direct and simple copy of socially organized processes; the point he made in his formulation of the general genetic law of cultural development about the transformations involved in internalization warns against any such view. What he is saying is that there is a close connection, grounded in genetic transitions, between the specific structures and processes of intermental and intramental functioning, which, in turn, implies that different forms of intermental functioning give rise to related differences in the forms of intramental functioning.

A second claim concerns the definition of higher mental functions (such as thinking, voluntary attention, and logical memory). The definition involved here is quite different from what psychologists usually have in mind when they speak of mental functions. Specifically, it assumes that the notion of mental function can properly be applied to social as well as individual forms of activity. This is the first of the two senses I referred to in Chapter 1 in which mind "extends beyond the skin." From this perspective, it is appropriate to predicate of dyads and other groups terms such as "think" and "remember." As David Middleton (1987) has noted, this point was being made by F. C. Bartlett (1935) in England at the same time that Vygotsky was writing in the Soviet Union, and it is being revived by investigators who have recently undertaken the study of "social memory" and "socially distributed cognition" (Hutchins, in press).

As an example of the kind of phenomena Vygotsky had in mind, let us consider the following case (Tharp and Gallimore, 1988):

> A 6-year-old child has lost a toy and asks her father for help. The father asks where she last saw the toy; the child says "I can't remember." He asks a series of questions—did you have it in your room? Outside? Next door? To each question, the child answers "no." When he says "in the car?", she says "I think so" and goes to retrieve the toy. (p. 14)

In such cases one cannot answer the question "Who did the remembering?" by pointing to either one person or the other. Instead, it is the dyad as a system that has carried out the function of remembering on the intermental plane. This same general point has also been made in connection with other aspects of mental functioning, such as problem solving (Wertsch, 1979a).

Vygotsky's general claim about the social origins of higher mental functioning in the individual surfaces most clearly in connection with the "zone of proximal development," a notion that has recently received a great deal of attention in the West (Brown and French, 1978; Cole, 1985; Rogoff and Wertsch, 1984; Tharp and Gallimore, 1988). This zone is defined as the distance between a child's "*actual developmental level as determined by independent problem solving*" and the higher level of "*potential development as determined through problem solving under adult guidance or in collaboration with more capable peers*" (1978, p. 86).

Vygotsky examined the implications of the zone of proximal development for the assessment of intelligence and for the organization of instruction. With regard to the former, he argued that measuring the level of potential development is just as important as measuring the actual developmental level; with regard to the latter, he argued that instruction should be tied more closely to the level of potential development than to the level of actual development. All these claims about the relationship between actual and potential levels of development reflect Vygotsky's more general concern with the intramental and intermental planes of mental functioning outlined in his general genetic law of cultural development.

Mediation

The third general theme that runs throughout Vygotsky's formulation of a sociocultural approach is the claim that higher mental functioning and human action in general are mediated by tools (or "technical tools") and signs (or "psychological tools"). Here again the influence of Marx and Engels is evident, especially in Vygotsky's discussion of the use of tools in the emergence of labor activity. But Vygotsky's main contribution resulted from his focus on psychological as opposed to technical tools. His lifelong interest in the complex processes of human semiotic action allowed him to bring great sophistication to the task of outlining the role of sign systems, such as human language, in intermental and intramental functioning.

An essential starting point in trying to understand Vygotsky's ideas about sign systems such as language, diagrams, and arithmetic is his assumption about the relationship between semiotic and other forms of action. As we saw in Chapter 1, this assumption distinguishes his approach from that of many others. In contrast to many contemporary analyses of language, which focus on the structure of sign systems independent of any mediating role they might play, Vygotsky approached language and other sign systems in terms of how they are a part of and *mediate* human action (thus his association with the term *mediated action*).

An example can be found in Vygotsky's analysis (1978) of the "forbidden colors task" studied by Leont'ev (1932). In this task children were asked a series of questions about the colors of objects, which they were to answer using color terms. According to the rules of the game, they were not to use certain color terms at all or any term more than once. They were given a set of colored cards and told that they could use these cards in any way they wished to assist their performance.

Vygotsky reported that preschool children (five to six years of age) often did not appreciate the mediational capacity of the cards, whereas older children (eight to thirteen years of age) employed them in various ways as memory aids. For example, some of the older children spread the colored cards out in front of them as they began the task. They then turned a colored card over whenever they used the corresponding color term: if they responded to a question using "red," they turned the red card in front of them face down so that this term would no longer be available for answering other questions. In contrast, preschool children often did not employ the cards in any systematic way, even though they stated that the cards had somehow helped them. In some cases Vygotsky reported that the cards actually hindered children's performance.

Vygotsky's analysis of the forbidden colors task reflects his tendency to approach signs in terms of their mediational properties rather than in terms of some kind of semantic analysis abstracted from any context of use. In his view, it is meaningless to assert that individuals "have" a sign, or have mastered it, without addressing the ways in which they do or do not use it to mediate their own actions or those of others.

Thus, his approach may be viewed as a particular version of a "use theory" of meaning (Strawson, 1971). Although it overlaps in certain essential ways with those approaches concerned with "pragmatics" or "discourse analysis," his focus on the mediational properties of semiotic processes means that this parallel is limited.

Also underlying Vygotsky's account of mediation is a set of assumptions about the nature of particular higher mental functions, more specifically, his view that thinking, voluntary attention, and logical memory form a system of "interfunctional relations" (Wertsch, 1985c). The importance of this issue for him is manifest in the first sentence of *Thinking and Speech,* his last, and probably most important, work. There, he noted that "the study of thought and language is one of the areas of psychology in which a clear understanding of interfunctional relations is particularly important" (1987, p. 1). He devoted the entire volume, in fact, to the issue of how speaking and thinking come to be thoroughly intertwined in human life, a cogent example of the interfunctional relationships that characterize human consciousness.

In examining the relationship between speech and thinking, Vygotsky's primary emphasis was on how different forms of speaking are related to different forms of thinking. Before going on to examine this relationship, however, a relationship that presupposes a widespread use of verbal mediation, it is worth at least noting another central assumption underlying the approach outlined by Vygotsky, that verbal mediational means would be used as widely and as often as possible.

This preference for verbal forms of mediation probably derived from two basic sources. First, it reflected Vygotsky's own cultural background: he grew up in an intellectual Russian Jewish family where the verbal formulation and resolution of problems was highly valued, and as an adult he continued to live and work in professional settings that placed a premium on verbal representation and verbal debate. Second, the formal instruction of literacy stood at the center of his theoretical and practical interests during the period when he produced most of his writings, and one of the hallmarks of formal instruction is, again, a strong preference for using verbal mediational means to represent and resolve a wide range of problems.

Vygotsky's assumptions about the efficacy and naturalness of verbal mediational means are shared by a great deal of research in the West on the development of mental functioning. These assumptions tend to go unnoticed except by investigators who have had experience with communicative and mental functioning in certain other sociocultural settings. Rogoff and her colleagues (1990) have noted, for example, that socialization practices in some nonwestern cultures involve much less reliance on verbal communication than is typical for western children. This is in no way a claim that such children are deprived of stimulation; it simply means that the forms of "guided participation" in which these children are involved rely much more extensively on nonverbal forms of communication and context manipulation than is typical in the lives of western children.

A particularly telling example of how children may differ in their tendency to use verbal mediation to solve problems can be found in the work of J. M. Kearins (1981, 1986). Kearins compared the performance of aboriginal children of desert origin on a series of visual spatial memory tasks with that of European "white" Australian children. Children from six to seventeen years of age were presented with different-colored items arrayed on a board and asked to recreate the array after the items had been placed together in a pile. Kearins documented consistently superior performances by aboriginal children on these tasks. Whereas the European Australian children tried to employ strategies grounded in verbal mediation, such as rehearsing lists of verbal labels, the aboriginal children showed very little evidence of employing verbal mediation strategies. Instead, they seemed to rely on visual strategies of a kind postulated as useful in desert way-finding.

Kearins's findings run counter to those of most such comparative studies. In contrast to the usual results, she found that aboriginal children consistently outperformed the European Australian children. The explanation is not that she found an unusual group of subjects but rather that she used a task that does not "privilege" verbal mediation strategies. Tasks that do privilege verbal mediation strategies have been at the core of a great deal of comparative research, and their use almost guarantees that subjects who do not automatically invoke such strategies will be at a disadvantage. Instead of jumping to the question of how effective subjects are at employing a particular verbal strategy, Kearins's studies suggest that, at least in some cases, it is appropriate to ask whether verbal strategies in general are useful.

Thus the findings of investigators such as Rogoff and Kearins reveal an ethnocentric bias, which underlies the ideas of Vygotsky and of many contemporary investigators concerned with the relationship between speech and thinking. This bias is not so much one that invalidates the research as it is one that limits the applicability of constructs to certain groups and settings. It reflects a pattern of privileging that distinguishes the performance of people functioning in various cultural, historical, and institutional settings.

In his analyses of mediation, Vygotsky relied heavily on the genetic method. He first examined some form of action, such as problem solving, and then introduced a new mediational means in an attempt to examine the resulting changes. This is the essence of his method of "dual stimulation," whose roots can be traced to his own ideas and to ideas in Luria's (1976b) early, "pre-Vygotskian" research on the "combined motor method."

An example of how the dual stimulation method guided Vygotsky's thinking can be found in early research with Luria and Leont'ev on patients with Parkinson's disease (reported by Radzikhovskii, 1979). In these studies, Vygotsky asked patients to perform various actions, such as walking across a room. In several cases, the patient's response was an increase in tremors. But when pieces of paper were laid out on the floor to indicate the sequence of steps the patient was to take and the patient was again asked to walk across the room, Luria and Leont'ev reported that, in some cases, at this point the patient's tremors decreased. The patient was able to walk across the room by treading sequentially on the pieces of paper.

As L. A. Radzikhovskii (1979) has noted, Vygotsky's explanation began with the fact that *two* sets of stimuli were involved: the verbal commands (stimuli that failed by themselves to generate the desired response) and the pieces of paper (stimuli that served to *mediate* the patient's response to the first set). This concern with the dynamics of dual stimulation also motivated the studies of children's performance on the forbidden colors task described above.

As Minick (1987) and Wertsch (1985c) have noted, during the last decade of his life Vygotsky shifted his focus from relatively simple "stimuli-means," such as of pieces of paper and colored cards, to more complex semiotic phenomena. Yet his basic approach—genetic analysis as reflected in the method of dual stimulation—continued to characterize his work.

The insight guiding this work was that the inclusion of signs in action fundamentally transforms the action. The incorporation of mediational means does not simply facilitate action that could have occurred without them; instead, as Vygotsky (1981a) noted, "by being included in the process of behavior, the psychological tool alters the entire flow and structure of mental functions. It does this by determining the structure of a new instrumental act, just as a technical tool alters the process of a natural adaptation by determining the form of labor operations" (p. 137).

The Shaping of Mediational Means   Focusing on mediational means touches on another important sense in which "mind goes beyond the skin": the agent of mediated action is seen as the individual or individuals *acting in conjunction with mediational means*. This general point has been recognized by several scholars. Building on a theoretical tradition quite different from Vygotsky's, Bateson (1972) presented the following illustration:

> Suppose I am a blind man, and I use a stick. I go tap, tap, tap. Where do *I* start? Is my mental system bounded at the handle of the stick? Is it bounded by my skin? Does it start halfway up the stick? Does it start at the tip of the stick? But these are nonsense questions. The stick is a pathway along which transformations of difference are being transmitted. The way to delineate the system is to draw the limiting line in such a way that you do not cut any of these pathways in ways which leave things inexplicable. (p. 459)

When a central role is attributed to mediational means, it becomes essential to specify the forces that shape them (and hence, mediated action). In the case of the stick used by the blind man, why does it have a particular length, color, and thickness? In the case of language, why does it have a particular set of structural properties when others are imaginable?

One's first inclination might be to assume that such properties have emerged or have been designed in response to the demands of individual psychological functioning. Vygotsky's analyses of the role of mediational means in dual stimulation are often consistent with this interpretation. The use of pieces of paper in the study of patients with Parkinson's disease and of colored cards in the forbidden colors task are cases in point. In both instances, mediational means were created with the express intent of shaping individual action.

Although individual—indeed, psychological—factors place certain limits on mediational means, the sociocultural approach I have been outlining suggests that cultural, historical, and institutional factors also play an essential role. In pursuing a line of reasoning that reflected their concern with Marxist claims about the primacy of social forces, Vygotsky and his colleagues made this very point. They contended that many of the design features of mediational means originate in social life. As stated by Luria (1981), *"in order to explain the highly complex forms of human consciousness one must go beyond the human organism. One must seek the origins of conscious activity and "categorical" behavior not in the recesses of the human brain or in the depths of the spirit, but in the external conditions of life. Above all, this means that one must seek these origins in the external processes of social life, in the social and historical forms of human existence"* (p. 25).

Although Vygotsky was clearly in accord with this general theoretical claim, his empirical studies of social processes were limited primarily to intermental functioning. In his view, the key to understanding forms of semiotic mediation on the intramental plane is to analyze their intermental origins, a point that is reflected in his claim that "a sign is always originally a means used for social purposes, a means of influencing others, and only later becomes a means of influencing oneself" (1981b, p. 157). Focusing more specifically on the sign system of language, he argued that "the primary function of speech, both for the adult and for the child, is the function of communication, social contact, influencing surrounding individuals" (1934a, p. 45).

One of the specific ways Vygotsky worked out these claims is in his account of "egocentric" and "inner" speech. Since these speech forms derive from "communication, social contact, influencing surrounding individuals," it follows that they should reflect certain properties of their intermental precursors, such as a dialogic structure. This is precisely what Vygotsky seems to have had in mind when he asserted that "egocentric speech . . . grows out of its social foundations by means of transferring social, collaborative forms of behavior to the sphere of the individual's psychological functioning" (1934a, p. 45).

In contrast to Vygotsky's conclusions about the forces that shape mediational means—which were usually limited to the dynamics of intermental functioning—the more general claim I would like to pursue is that mediational means emerge in response to a wide range of social forces. Specifically, forces other than those of localized intermental functioning may be involved. Because Vygotsky and his colleagues were influenced by Marxist theory, one would expect their account to extend to broader historical and economic forces; this seems to be precisely what motivated Luria's concern with "the social and historical forms of human existence." But Vygotsky and his colleagues did relatively little to elaborate this claim in concrete ways.

As an illustration of this point, let us consider the functioning of an object that is mediating my action as I write, the keyboard of a personal computer. The configuration of this keyboard stems from the work of its designer, Christopher Latham Sholes. In 1872 Sholes arrived at a layout representing a compromise between several demands. One had to do with the mechanics of typewriter keys. Early versions of his machines were "slower" than typists' fingers, so the keys constantly jammed. Sholes's solution was to redesign the keyboard in an effort to slow the typist down. As William Hoffer (1985) has reported, the most common letters—E, T, O, A, N, I—became widely distributed, frequent combinations such as ED were arranged so that they had to be struck by the same finger, and the typist was required to use the weaker left hand 57 percent of the time. The familiar "QWERTY" keyboard that resulted was thus specifically designed to insure a kind of inefficiency.

In 1936 August Dvořák, a distant cousin of Czech composer Antonín Dvořák, devised a new keyboard. Using the well-known principles of time and motion studies, namely, simple motion, short movement, and rhythmic sequence, Dvořák created a keyboard grounded in the very principles of efficiency that Sholes had sought to avoid: "All five vowels and the five most common consonants are on the center, or 'home' row—right under the fingertips. With those letters—A, O, E, U, I, D, H, T, N, S—the typist can produce nearly 4,000 common English words (compared with about 100 on QWERTY's home row). Seventy percent of typing is done on the home row" (Hoffer, 1985, p. 38). For those familiar with the Dvořák keyboard the benefits are obvious. In study after study it has consistently proved to be faster and much easier to use than the QWERTY keyboard; every time an international typing speed record has been set in recent years, it has been on a Dvořák keyboard.

Even this brief comparison reveals something about the power of historical context in shaping mediational means. The QWERTY keyboard, in one sense purposefully inefficient, has retained its position of dominance even though the original rationale for its use has long since disappeared. For several decades, the improved technology of typewriters and now the capabilities of electronic keyboards have obviated the need for it. In the case of a personal computer, a set of key caps and a relatively simple program will convert a QWERTY keyboard to a Dvořák configuration. In addition, studies have consistently demonstrated that those trained on the QWERTY system can master the much more efficient Dvořák system after about twenty hours of practice, and users report that it is not difficult to switch back and forth between the two. Yet, as this example makes clear, mediational means often emerge in response to requirements other than the efficiency of intra-mental or intermental functioning.

In most cases there is no direct conflict between the demands for efficiency and inefficiency in mediational means. Furthermore, media-tional means are not generally the product of conscious design. None-theless, the case of the QWERTY keyboard provides useful insights about the general point I wish to make here: the mediational means that shape mediated action typically do not emerge in response to the demands of this action, either on the intermental or the intramental plane.

As a second illustration of this general claim, I want to turn to sociological studies of problem solving in bureaucratic settings. These studies (Cicourel, 1981; Knorr-Cetina, 1981; Latour and Woolgar, 1986; Mehan, 1989, 1990) have focused on a variety of ways in which discourse and psychological processes are shaped by their institutional settings. Hugh Mehan (1989, 1990), for example, has carried out extensive research on how bureaucratic structures and processes in schools sort students into categories such as "normal," "special," "learning disabled," and "educationally handicapped." He begins his analysis of how school systems derive "clarity from ambiguity" on this issue with the general assumption that "events in the world are ambiguous. We struggle to understand these events, to imbue them with meaning. The choice of a particular way of representing events gives them a particular meaning" (1989, p. 1). About the procedures used in the institutional setting of schools to decide whether students are "normal" or "special," Mehan notes that "while this activity is as old as schools themselves, in response to recently enacted state and federal legislation, this classification and sorting activity has become more formalized. There are now procedures mandated by law, espe-cially PL 94-142, 'The Education for All Handicapped Students Act,' concerning the referral of students to special education" (p. 2).

A major implication of these legal procedures is that each student, with all of his or her unique particularities, must be considered in terms of a set of explicit, institutionally defined categories. As in the case of all mediational means, these categories, and the procedures for employing them, play a fundamental role in shaping intermental and intramental functioning. Here, instead of simply reflecting or describ-ing some kind of reality about a particular student, they "constitute" or "construct" (Mehan, 1989) the identity of that student in accordance with socioculturally situated assumptions.

Among these assumptions, Mehan (1989) points to the "medicalization" of children's difficulties in schools. Rather than considering a learning disability as a socioculturally situated and constructed category, this procedure assumes that it is a property intrinsic to the individual—a disorder caused by central nervous system dysfunction or a hereditary condition. It is the generally accepted "prevalence of the psychological idiom" (Mehan, 1989) that gives psychologists on Eligibility and Placement committees particular power in classifying students.

Although one might assume that standardized psychological assessment procedures would produce classifications based solely on students' objective characteristics, there is evidence that the categories used by Eligibility and Placement committees reflect other factors as well. Specifically, they are employed to define students at least partly in accordance with a system of financial incentives set by the institutional setting itself. As Mehan notes, the federal government provides supplementary funding to support special education for a certain percentage of the student body. This funding is available for students in "pullout" and "whole day" special education programs in the school district but not for those sent outside the district. In Mehan's view, "the fact that there were *no* out of district placements during the year we studied the Coast district makes sense when placed against this background" (1989, p. 23). Such facts do not indicate some kind of conspiracy or even a conscious decision; they derive from the institutionally situated categories and the patterns of speaking and thinking employed by the teachers, psychologists, administrators, and parents on Eligibility and Placement committees.

Considered from the general perspective of mediational means, the processes used in sorting students are similar in several ways to the QWERTY keyboard. First, they are fundamentally shaped by the mediational means they employ. Just as the keyboard was determined by the capabilities of the machine, the discussion and deliberation of Eligibility and Placement committees occur within the constraints of the institutionally provided categories. Second, the power of mediational means in organizing action is often not consciously recognized by those who use them, which contributes to the belief that cultural tools are the product of natural or necessary factors rather than of concrete sociocultural forces. When asked why the QWERTY keyboard is organized as it is, and most people do not spontaneously ask themselves, most users respond that it was designed to insure efficiency. Mehan's finding that members of Eligibility and Placement committees seldom, if ever, questioned the categories they used also reflects this unconscious acceptance of the naturalness or necessity of the mediational means involved. And third, because mediational means are products of cultural, historical, and institutional forces that may have little obvious relevance to the local settings in which they are employed, they shape these settings in ways that might otherwise not be deemed appropriate from the perspective of intermental or intramental functioning. It is certainly not always the case, as with the QWERTY keyboard, that the mediational means are specifically designed to make a form of action inefficient, but the forces that shape mediational means typically introduce unintended effects into mediated action. From a theoretical perspective that sees agency as *mediated,* this fact assumes major importance.

Semiotic Potentials This view of how mediational means emerge in response to various sociocultural forces has several implications. Most important, it implies that mediational means have a predisposition to be used more easily for certain purposes than for others, and it implies that this predisposition may not be based on ideal or maximally efficient forms of individual mental action. In the case of language, this is not to assert that certain concepts or forms of reasoning are made impossible by the use of particular expressions. Such a rigid view has sometimes been attributed to Whorf (1956) and Sapir (1931), but careful analysis of their writings (Lucy, in press) has shown this to be unfounded. It does mean, however, that certain patterns of speaking and thinking are easier, or come to be viewed as more appropriate in a specific setting than others. It is this issue that I shall address under the heading of "semiotic potentials" (Wertsch, 1985c).

At least in passing, Vygotsky recognized many semiotic potentials in language, but he focused on two in particular, which correspond to two genetic transitions he examined in some empirical detail: the development of concepts and the transition from social to egocentric to inner speech. In the case of concept development, Vygotsky was concerned with a semiotic potential that is realized in the "decontextualization of mediational means" (Wertsch, 1985c). This decontextualization process results in the mastery of abstract forms of reasoning associated with the kinds of tasks found in formal schooling in which linguistic units are abstracted from their communicative contexts and become objects of reflection. One of Vygotsky's major concerns was the "scientific" or "academic" concepts that are grounded in particular sorts of semiotic activity (for example, making definitions) as opposed to the "everyday" concepts grounded in children's concrete experience. In the former, the focus is on ways in which words and other linguistic units are related to one another independent of their relationship with extralinguistic reality, whereas in the case of everyday concepts, the focus is on the relationship between linguistic unit and concrete, extra-linguistic experience.

The semiotic action associated with scientific concepts is decontextualized because it focuses on forms and meanings that remain constant across speech event contexts. In no sense is semiotic action itself decontextualized; indeed, "decontextualized action" would be a contradiction in terms. What is decontextualized are the mediational means, which have come to be treated as abstract objects of reflection rather than as embedded in the context of other forms of intermental or intramental action.

As an example, let us consider the abstract definitions found in dictionaries. These definitions focus on those aspects of word meaning that are assumed to exist independent of specific usage. In creating a definition, an equivalence relationship such as "ophthalmologist = eye doctor" is assumed to remain constant, regardless of the particular communicative context in which "ophthalmologist" might be used. This does not mean that definitions produce direct insight into some underlying, "real" meaning of words; the groundlessness of this assumption has been revealed by Linell (1982, 1988), Rommetveit (1988), and others. Instead, there is a particular form of semiotic action, a "discourse mode" or a "speech genre," in which linguistic units are understood as abstracted from individual communicative contexts. In this connection it is appropriate to speak of "decontextualized mediational means" (Wertsch, 1985c).

In contrast to his account of scientific concepts, in which he focused on decontextualization, Vygotsky's analysis of the formation of inner speech focused on the semiotic potential of human language for increased contextualization. Specifically, he was concerned with ways in which speech comes to serve as its own context. Because this involves a new kind of context, which exists alongside other, already extant contexts, it might be more appropriate to speak in this connection of "recontextualization."

In this process of recontextualization, the interpretation of utterances depends increasingly on the linguistic information in the texts in which they are embedded. An example is the phenomenon of anaphora. Anaphora refers to the linguistic relationship between referring expressions, such as "he," "she," and "it," and the preceding linguistic context, which makes it possible to identify the referent of such expressions. Consider the pronominal referring expression "he" in the following text: "I saw a strange man the other day. He was very tall." In order to interpret what "he" refers to, one must rely on the linguistic context provided by the first sentence in the text; the interpretation of "he" depends on the fact that it is "coreferential" (Hickmann, 1985) with "a strange man." If the second sentence in this text were preceded by a different sentence ("I saw a giraffe at the zoo"), the referent of "he" would change.

Anaphora is just one of the many phenomena that might be considered under the heading of linguistic contextualization. As investigators such as Maya Hickmann (1985) and Annette Karmiloff-Smith (1979) have noted, the mastery of anaphora is a relatively late achievement in childhood, not being complete until early adolescence. This is consistent with its involvement in the development of inner speech.

Vygotsky's account of inner speech was influenced by the ideas of several other figures. Various notions of inner speech were developed by scholars in prerevolutionary Russia and the USSR (Potebnya, 1913; Voloshinov, 1973), and its existence and utility were widely accepted among Soviet scholars. But the particular impetus for Vygotsky's analysis of inner speech was provided by the account of egocentric speech outlined by Piaget (1923). Piaget viewed egocentric speech as one of several phenomena that reflect the general egocentricity, or solipsism, of young children. In pursuing his research on this topic, he produced extensive empirical data as well as a set of categories for understanding and coding these data.

Vygotsky clearly recognized the "indisputable and enormous credit" owed to Piaget for his account of egocentric speech, but he took issue with Piaget over its function and its fate. He saw it not as a reflection, or a symptom, of children's underlying egocentricity, but rather, as a speech form that served a cognitive, self-regulative function (Levina, 1981). According to Vygotsky, the appearance of egocentric speech marked the emerging differentiation of speech functions: "in the process of growth the child's social speech, which is multifunctional, develops in accordance with the principle of the differentiation of separate functions, and at a certain age is quite sharply differentiated into egocentric and communicative speech" (1934a, p. 45).

With regard to its fate, Vygotsky argued that as speech functions become increasingly differentiated, egocentric speech "goes underground," or is transformed into inner speech. It serves as "a transitional form from external to internal speech" (1934a, p. 464). To test his hypotheses about the function and fate of egocentric speech Vygotsky (1934a) conducted a series of empirical studies (see Wertsch [1985c] for reviews of these and related studies). The results generally corroborated his own claims rather than Piaget's. Subsequent research by other investigators (Bivens and Berk, 1990; Goudena, 1983, 1987; Kohlberg, Yaeger, and Hjertholm, 1968) has lent further support to Vygotsky's interpretation of this phenomenon.

In his account of egocentric and inner speech, Vygotsky identified two categories of properties: "syntactic" and "semantic." These properties represent the ways in which the structure and function of these speech forms differ from those of speech in social communication. The "first and most important" syntactic property of inner speech is its unique abbreviated syntax. As with all the properties of inner speech, he argued that it is possible to examine empirically the emergence of this abbreviated syntax in the development of egocentric speech and thus to gain insight into the "fragmentary, abbreviated nature of inner speech as compared to external speech" (1934a, p. 292).

The main way in which the syntax of egocentric and inner speech comes to be abbreviated is through "predicativity": "As it develops, egocentric speech does not manifest a simple tendency toward abbreviation and the omission of words; it does not manifest a simple transition toward a telegraphic style. Rather, it shows a quite unique tendency toward abbreviating phrases and sentences by preserving the predicate and associated parts of the sentence at the expense of deleting the subject and other words associated with it" (1934a, p. 293).

As I have noted elsewhere (Wertsch, 1979b), Vygotsky's account of predicativity is based on a functional analysis of utterances in context rather than an analysis of decontextualized sentence types. It is thus concerned with the kind of issue outlined previously in connection with anaphora. In general, what this means is that those parts of an utterance dealing with information that can be assumed to be understood can be "attenuated" (Chafe, 1974, 1976). In the case of anaphora, a pronoun can replace a longer noun phrase ("he" instead of "a strange man"); in other cases, surface form may be deleted entirely.

Vygotsky's analysis of the semantic properties of inner speech rested on his formulation of the notion of "sense" (*smysl*) as opposed to "meaning" (*znachenie*).

> The sense of a word . . . is the aggregate of all the psychological facts emerging in our consciousness because of this word. Therefore, the sense of a word always turns out to be a dynamic, flowing, complex formation which has several zones of differential stability . . . As we know, a word readily changes its sense in various contexts. Conversely, its meaning is that fixed, unchanging point which remains stable during all the changes of sense in various contexts. This change in a word's sense is a basic fact to be accounted for in the semantic analysis of speech. The real meaning of a word is not constant. In one operation a word emerges in one meaning and in another it takes on another meaning. (1934a, p. 305)

According to Vygotsky, in inner speech, sense predominates over meaning, and it is likewise possible to examine this tendency through the study of egocentric speech.

One of the correlates of Vygotsky's belief in the predominance of sense over meaning is that egocentric and inner speech have unique organizational and combinatorial properties. In addition to being manifested in syntactic properties (for example, predicativity) these properties are also characteristic of semantic organization. Vygotsky addressed the unique possibilities for coordinating units of sense under the headings "agglutination" and the "influx of sense." With regard to agglutination, he wrote that "first, in entering into the composition of a complex word, separate words often undergo abbreviation in sound such that only part of them becomes part of the complex word; second, the resulting complex word that expresses an extremely complex concept emerges as a structurally and functionally unified word, not as a combination of independent words" (1934a, p. 307). Such comments are obviously grounded in the ideas of such scholars as Karl Buhler, who developed linguistic typologies that would include agglutinative, or synthetic, languages.

With regard to the influx of sense, Vygotsky argued that units of egocentric and inner speech reflect more fluid and dynamic combinatorial possibilities than are found in social speech. As opposed to social speech, where more stable forms of meaning predominate, in egocentric and inner speech a word's sense is influenced and changed as a function of its entering into an intralinguistic context: "in inner speech the word, as it were, absorbs the sense of preceding and subsequent words, thereby extending almost without limit the boundaries of its meaning" (1934a, p. 308). As will become evident in later chapters, Vygotsky's notion of the influx of sense provides a major link with Bakhtin's account of dialogicality and with analyses of socialization into a sociocultural milieu.

Vygotsky and the Whorfian Hypothesis

If there is one name popularly associated in the West with the notion that language influences thought, it is that of Benjamin Lee Whorf (1956). Following the lead of his intellectual mentors, Boas (1916, 1966) and Sapir (1921, 1931), Whorf developed a complex set of ideas about the ways in which the structure of a language shapes the habitual thought patterns of its speakers. The ideas of Whorf are sometimes associated with those of Vygotsky (Schieffelin and Ochs, 1986), and there are indeed some interesting connections between the two thinkers. Yet there are also major differences, which make their views complementary rather than identical.

In this case there is an actual historical connection via Sapir (Lee, 1985). Echoing Sapir directly at several points Vygotsky (1934a) wrote, "In order to transmit some experience or content of consciousness to another person, there is no other way than to ascribe the content to a known class, to a known group of phenomena, and as we know, this necessarily involves generalization. Thus it turns out that social interaction necessarily presupposes generalization and the development of word meaning, that is, generalization becomes possible in the presence of the development of social interaction. Thus higher, uniquely human forms of psychological social interaction are possible only because human thinking reflects reality in a generalized way" (pp. 11–12).

Although Vygotsky draws on the work of Sapir, this does not mean that his views corresponded in general with those of Boas, Sapir, or Whorf. Indeed, he differed from these other theorists in several essential ways. The first concerns the place of genetic analysis. Vygotsky's heavy reliance on this particular form of analysis, especially his comments on the nature of sociocultural history (as reflecting a development from "primitive" to modern peoples), contrasts sharply with the Boas-Sapir-Whorf tradition. As noted by Lucy and Wertsch (1987), "Boas's central concern was to challenge the nineteenth-century evolutionary approaches in social science which understood so-called primitive peoples and their culture as representing various stages in a unilinear development toward modern European racial and social forms" (p. 72).

A second difference concerns the role of grammatical analysis. Vygotsky may have cited Sapir, but this reflects neither a general congruence in their ideas about how to conduct linguistic analysis nor agreement on the fundamental question of the unit of linguistic analysis that offered an appropriate starting point. Indeed, in his research Vygotsky (1934a) selected word meaning as the unit of analysis, whereas Sapir and Whorf focused on the proposition or its linguistically encoded form, the sentence (Silverstein, 1987). This difference is, in part, a result of the languages these researchers examined: Vygotsky focused on Indo-European languages in which lexemes are relatively clear and easily distinguished, while Whorf and his colleagues examined languages whose structure obscures the boundaries between lexemes and sentences.

Their choice of analytic units also reflects major differences in the kinds of linguistic analyses Vygotsky and Whorf carried out. Whorf's focus on the sentence is closely tied to his overriding concern with grammatical structure. As Lucy (1987) noted in his comprehensive review of the Boas-Sapir-Whorf tradition, this grammatical focus clearly characterized Whorf's approach, even though he occasionally used lexical examples to introduce his general argument.

A third difference between Whorf and Vygotsky concerns their assumptions about language functions. According to Lucy (1987), "Whorf assumed that language was essentially referential in nature, that is, that it primarily fulfilled a referential function" (p. 125), an assumption that has inspired criticism and motivated several attempts to expand on these ideas by considering "functional," as well as "structural" relativity (Hymes, 1966; Ochs, 1988). In contrast, Vygotsky's notion of function and his claims about different functions played an essential role in his semiotic analysis. He considered form-function relationships and "functional differentiation," and he was concerned with "social" versus "individual" functions, "communicative" versus "intellectual" functions, "indicative" versus "symbolic" functions, and so forth (Wertsch, 1985c).

The general upshot of such Vygotsky-Whorf comparisons (see also Lucy and Wertsch, 1987) is that in their treatment of the relationship between language and thought the two theorists differ in important ways. These differences are attributable in part to the fact that Vygotsky focused primarily on psychological issues, whereas Whorf was concerned primarily with linguistic analysis. In some cases, such as the role of genetic analysis, the difference seems to be in the form of a clear-cut contradiction. Even here, however, there may be more similarity than at first meets the eye, depending on how one interprets Vygotsky's ideas about elementary mental functioning and Whorf's claims about the nature of the mental processes that are affected by language use.

In other cases, the difference is clearly one of complementarity rather than contradiction. Whorf's selection of the sentence as a unit of analysis allowed him to see a number of issues in language structure that Vygotsky, with his focus on the word, did not appreciate. As I have argued elsewhere (Wertsch, 1985c), this is an area where Vygotskian analyses of semiotic analyses could benefit from incorporating Whorfian insights. In the case of the role of language function, however, clearly Vygotsky has something to offer Whorf.

3

Beyond Vygotsky: Bakhtin's Contribution

> We do not want to be Ivans who have forgotten their heritage; we do not
> suffer from a delusion of grandeur, thinking that history begins with us; we
> do not want to obtain from history a clean but trivial name; we want a name
> on which the dust of centuries will settle. In this we see our historical right,
> our historical role, our goal of realizing psychology as a science.
>
> —Vygotsky, *Problems of General Psychology*

Vygotsky's analysis of higher mental functioning provides a
foundation for a sociocultural approach to mediated action.
In this connection, his investigation of the social origins of individual
mental functioning and his claims about semiotic mediation are particularly important. Yet in certain essential respects he did not succeed
in providing a genuinely sociocultural approach to mind. In particular,
he did little to spell out how specific historical, cultural, and institutional settings are tied to various forms of mediated action.

This limitation is one of several in Vygotsky's analysis of the social
processes underlying individual mental functioning. In his account of
intermental processes Vygotsky focused on small group interaction,
especially the interaction of the adult-child dyad. His ideas about the
general genetic law of cultural development, the zone of proximal
development, and the various forms of semiotic mediation involved
all tended to rest on analyses of this type of "interindividual" (Shotter,
1982) interaction. What is somewhat ironic for someone interested in
formulating a Marxist psychology, he made precious little mention
of broader historical, institutional, or cultural processes such as class
struggle, alienation, and the rise of commodity fetishism.

A major reason for Vygotsky's failure to deal with broader sociocultural issues may be that his research was cut short by his death from
tuberculosis at the age of thirty-seven. In my opinion, this point is
made too often in trying to explain why Vygotsky did not deal with
particular issues. In many cases there is no reason to believe that he
ever would have dealt with a particular issue. Yet in this case the point
has some relevance because there are indications in Vygotsky's late

writings that he was moving toward considering how the mental functioning of the individual is linked to cultural, historical, and institutional contexts.

A key link between sociocultural setting and individual mental functioning from a Vygotskian point of view is the way in which various forms of mediated intermental functioning are related to sociocultural contexts. This point has been noted by Vygotsky scholars such as Norris Minick. In his analysis of Vygotsky's approach Minick (1985) argues that "the links between dyadic or small group interactions and the broader socio-cultural system must be recognized and explored . . . [A]ctions are at one and the same time components of the life of the individual and the social system. This point is as crucial for the analysis of the development of intermental actions as it is for the analysis of the development of intramental actions. No less than the action of an individual, the action of a dyad or small group is a component in the social system. Correspondingly, the intermental actions and the social interaction that makes that action possible will be defined and structured in certain respects by the broader social and cultural system" (p. 257).

The specific sociocultural setting of increasing concern to Vygotsky in his later writings was that of formal schooling. A comparison of Chapters 5 and 6 in *Thinking and Speech* (1987) reveals this shift in his thinking. Both deal with the ontogenetic transition from "complexes" to "genuine," or "scientific," concepts, a transition that is one instantiation of the "decontextualization of mediational means" (Wertsch, 1985c). The two chapters differ, however, in what they see as the relevant developmental forces. In Chapter 5, which was based on research with Shif (1935) and written in the early 1930s, concept development is treated primarily in terms of individual psychology, that is, children's conceptual development as they move from "unorganized heaps" to "complexes" to "concepts." In Chapter 6, written in 1934, there is an essential change in the way Vygotsky approached these issues. He clearly continued to be interested in intramental functioning, but he now approached concept development from the perspective of how it emerges in institutionally situated activity. Because he was concerned with how the forms of speaking encountered in the social institution of formal schooling provide the framework within which concept development occurs, he focused on the forms of teacher-child intermental functioning in this setting rather than on children's intramental functioning alone.

The ideas he set out in Chapter 6 also give some sense of the direction Vygotsky's work was taking toward the end of his life. Because he made only a beginning, his writing lacks any detailed explication, but the trend is clear and suggests a concrete way to extend his ideas. It suggests, in short, that in order to formulate a more comprehensive sociocultural approach to mental functioning one should identify historically, culturally, and institutionally situated forms of mediated action and specify how their mastery leads to particular forms of mediated action on the intramental plane. This amounts to extending Vygotsky's ideas to bring the sociocultural situatedness of mediated action on the intermental plane to the fore. It is the sociocultural situatedness of mediated action that provides the essential link between the cultural, historical, and institutional setting on the one hand and the mental functioning of the individual on the other, and it is in this connection that Bakhtin's ideas are relevant.

Bakhtin's Contribution

Mikhail Mikhailovich Bakhtin's life, like those of many people in the Soviet Union of his time, was complex and difficult. In 1929 he was arrested for political crimes whose nature is not entirely clear. This arrest, which occurred in the early stages of Stalin's massive and brutal repression, resulted in Bakhtin's internal exile. Yet as Clark and Holquist (1984) have noted, his early arrest coupled with his chronic ill health proved to be his good fortune, since he was not sent to certain death in the harsher conditions of other camps. As a consequence, however, Bakhtin often could not publish his own writings, and a great deal of debate and confusion has ensued over who actually wrote several works attributed variously to him and to others.

Another reason for this confusion is that during his early career Bakhtin belonged to various intellectual collectives in which members worked, lived, and wrote together. As noted by a number of scholars (Clark and Holquist [1984], Morson [1986], Morson and Emerson [1989, in press], Titunik [1986], Titunik and Bruss [1976], and Todorov [1984]), this collaboration produced a set of manuscripts, published under the names of Bakhtin, P. N. Medvedev, and V. N. Voloshinov, whose individual authorship is not clear.

Some, such as Gary Saul Morson and Caryl Emerson (1989, in press), have argued that a clear distinction can be made between the works of Bakhtin (1981, 1984, 1986) and those of Medvedev (1978) and Voloshinov (1973). Among the important issues involved here is the fact that Voloshinov was a Marxist, whereas Bakhtin "quite demonstrably was not" (Emerson, 1989, p. 2). This difference becomes quite clear when one considers Bakhtin's focus on dialogicality, for example, a process he envisioned as being quite distinct from any kind of Hegelian or Marxist dialectic.

Furthermore, as Emerson (1989) has noted, Voloshinov, who focused on signs and sign systems, was concerned with issues that clearly fall under a relatively standard definition of semiotics. In contrast, "Bakhtin uses the word 'znak' [sign] and/or 'sign system' *very* rarely in his writings—three or four times in the material that has been published" (p. 2). According to Emerson, it may be appropriate to label Bakhtin a semiotician only if one accepts the definition V. V. Ivanov (1974) proposed in an article about Bakhtin. Here, Ivanov praised Bakhtin for initiating "semiotics in its present-day form," that is, semiotics which acknowledges that "the most important thing for making sense of meaning is not the sign, but the whole utterance into whose composition the sign enters" (p. 237).

In contrast, scholars such as Clark and Holquist (1984) have argued that there is a great deal of evidence to support the claim that Bakhtin was the primary, if not the sole, author of disputed texts published under the names of Voloshinov (1973) and Medvedev (1978). In their view, this does not preclude the possibility that Bakhtin wrote a basic text and that others modified and extended it before publishing it under their own names. They base their argument on textual analysis, the forms of argumentation employed, and the comments of Bakhtin and Bakhtin's wife.

Here, I shall assume that Bakhtin was heavily involved in the authorship of the disputed texts. This does not mean that he actually put pen to paper in the case of each part of each manuscript, but it does mean that his influence is very much in evidence. I take this middle position for two reasons. First, despite a great deal of scholarship, there is no clear answer to this question, and I am not in a position to add to the debate. Second, for quite principled reasons it may be that the issue, at least as it is usually formulated, *should* remain unresolved. In Bakhtin's view, the notion of sole, isolated authorship is a bogus one. An essential aspect of his construct of dialogicality is that multiple authorship is a necessary fact about all texts, written or spoken.

The one point where taking the middle ground may strike some as quite unsatisfying is that of the debt of these various authors to Marx. As I have argued above and elsewhere (Wertsch, 1985c), several ideas in Vygotsky's writings are clearly grounded in Marxist texts. In the case of works such as *Marxism and the Philosophy of Language* (Voloshinov, 1973), there is also an obvious connection to such texts. In the final analysis, however, it seems to me that there is little that is necessarily Marxist in either Vygotsky's or Voloshinov's writings. In both cases the facts of each author's biography suggest that Marxist ideas played an important role in giving rise to their claims, but their crucial arguments are not uniquely and necessarily indebted to Marx.

The Role of Utterance

Unlike many scholars of language, especially contemporary linguists who concern themselves primarily with linguistic form and meaning abstracted from the actual conditions of use, Bakhtin focused his analytic efforts on the *utterance,* "the *real unit* of speech communication." Bakhtin's insistence on examining the utterance is strikingly consistent with the focus on mediated action outlined in Chapter 1 in that it focuses on situated action rather than on objects that can be derived from analytic abstractions. In this connection Bakhtin wrote that "speech can exist in reality only in the form of concrete utterances of individual speaking people, speech subjects. Speech is always cast in the form of an utterance belonging to a particular speaking subject, and outside this form it cannot exist" (1986, p. 71).

As Clark and Holquist (1984) have noted, this focus on utterance does not mean Bakhtin rejected the notion that there is constancy and systematicity in speech. Instead, he viewed the utterance as the site at which this constancy and systematicity enter into contact and struggle with unique, situated performance. It was the unit of analysis that allowed him to ask, "Can the requirement of language for fixed meanings be yoked together with the no less urgent need of language users for meanings that can be various in the countless different contexts created by the flux of everyday life?" (Clark and Holquist, 1984, p. 10).

Thus Bakhtin readily accepted the need to study "the specific object of linguistics, something arrived at through a completely legitimate and necessary abstraction from various aspects of the concrete life of the word" (Bakhtin, 1984, p. 181). But because it focuses on units such as words and sentences (that is, units abstracted from actual use), he argued that linguistics alone cannot provide an adequate account of utterances. In his view the study of utterances requires an approach that transcends the concerns of individual existing disciplines, an approach that he termed "translinguistics."*

Translinguistics, according to Bakhtin, is "the study of those aspects in the life of the word, not yet shaped into separate and specific disciplines, that exceed—and completely legitimately—the boundaries of linguistics" (p. 181). Although Bakhtin never provided a comprehensive statement of what translinguistics would encompass, his comments indicate that it overlaps with the study of what today is called "pragmatics" or "discourse" (Sherzer, 1987). But no easy definitions are possible using such contemporary terms because he grounded translinguistics in the categories of *voice* and *dialogicality*.

Voice

In Bakhtin's account the notion of utterance is inherently linked with that of voice, or "the speaking personality, the speaking consciousness" (Holquist and Emerson, 1981, p. 434) This is so first of all because an utterance can exist only by being produced by a voice: "An utterance, spoken or written, is always expressed from a point of view [a voice], which for Bakhtin is a process rather than a location. Utterance is an activity that enacts differences in values. On an elementary level, for instance, the same words can mean different things depending on the particular intonation with which they are uttered in a specific context: intonation is the sound that value makes" (Clark and Holquist, 1984, p. 10).

As I noted in Chapter 1, for Bakhtin the notion of voice cannot be reduced to an account of vocal-auditory signals. Although he was often interested in the concrete qualities of voice quality, his account of the speaking consciousness is more general. It applies to written as well as spoken communication, and it is concerned with the broader issues of a speaking subject's perspective, conceptual horizon, intention, and world view.

Throughout his analysis Bakhtin stressed the idea that voices always exist in a social milieu; there is no such thing as a voice that exists in

---

*Bakhtin's actual term was "metalinguistics." Because of the numerous meanings attached to this term in contemporary studies of language and because, as Clark and Holquist (1984) have noted, the term *meta-* has become so banal in Western scholarship, I shall follow their lead and use the term "translinguistics."

total isolation from other voices. For example, in addition to the voice producing an utterance, the point of view or speaking consciousness being addressed was also fundamental. His concern with the processes by which voices engage one another highlights another point of correspondence with the action orientation outlined in Chapter 1. From Bakhtin's treatment of meaning, it is evident that he viewed it as an active process rather than as a static entity. He insisted at many points that meaning can come into existence only when two or more voices come into contact: when the voice of a listener responds to the voice of a speaker. His insistence on taking both voices into account reflects his concern with "addressivity, the quality of turning to someone else." In the absence of addressivity, "the utterance does not and cannot exist" (1986, p. 99).

Like utterance and voice, addressivity is clearly a phenomenon of *speech* as opposed to *language* and hence part of translinguistic as opposed to linguistic analysis. The units of analysis (such as words and sentences) used in linguistics "belong to nobody and are addressed to nobody. Moreover, they in themselves are devoid of any kind of relation to the other's utterance, the other's word. If an individual word or sentence is directed at someone, addressed to someone, then we have a completed utterance that consists of one word or one sentence, and addressivity is inherent not in the unit of language, but in the utterance" (p. 99). Bakhtin's concern with addressivity is grounded in his more general observation that "any utterance is a link in the chain of speech communication" (p. 84), an observation that, in turn, leads to his claim that "utterances are not indifferent to one another, and are not self-sufficient; they are aware of and mutually reflect one another" (p. 91).

There are several ways in which this view of speech communication manifests itself in Bakhtin's writings. For example, understanding or comprehending an utterance according to Bakhtin involves a process, one in which other utterances come into contact with and confront it: "For each word of the utterance that we are in the process of understanding, we, as it were, lay down a set of our own answering words. The greater their number and weight, the deeper and more substantial our understanding will be. Thus each of the distinguishable significative elements of an utterance and the entire utterance as a whole entity are translated in our minds into another active and responsive context . . . Understanding strives to match the speaker's word with a *counter word*" (Voloshinov, 1973, p. 102).

The addressee's voice is also involved in the chain of speech communication in as much as the speaking voice may indicate an awareness of it and reflect it in the very production of utterances. In this connection, Bakhtin noted that "every utterance must be regarded primarily as a *response* to preceding utterances of the given sphere (we understand the word 'response' here in the broadest sense)" (1986, p. 91). The responses he had in mind may take several forms: they may involve the speaker's quoting another voice, processes of abbreviation, such as those outlined in Chapter 2 in connection with inner speech, processes such as the formulation of an argument in order to circumvent counterarguments anticipated from other voices, and so forth.

Furthermore, Bakhtin did not limit the notion of addressee to only those speakers in the immediate speech situation. Instead, the voice or voices to which an utterance is addressed may be temporally, spatially, and socially distant: "This addressee can be an immediate participant-interlocutor in an everyday dialogue, a differentiated collective of specialists in some particular area of cultural communication, a more or less differentiated public, ethnic group, contemporaries, like-minded people, opponents and enemies, a subordinate, a superior, someone who is lower, higher, familiar, foreign, and so forth. And it can also be an indefinite, unconcretized *other*" (1986, p. 95).

Ultimately, an utterance reflects not only the voice producing it but also the voices to which it is addressed. In the formulation of an utterance a voice responds in some way to previous utterances and anticipates the responses of other, succeeding ones; when it is understood, an utterance comes into contact with the "counter word" of those who hear it.

Bakhtin's concern with addressivity in the utterance thus involves both a concern with *who is doing the speaking*—the fact that "the utterance has . . . an author" (1986, p. 95)—and a concern with *who is being addressed*. Because any utterance entails the idea of addressivity, utterances are inherently associated with at least two voices.

Dialogicality and Multivoicedness

That addressivity involves at least two voices reflects Bakhtin's concern with the most basic theoretical construct in his approach—dialogicality. It is most basic because it analytically precedes other constructs such as utterance and voice; the latter can be adequately understood only by invoking the notion of dialogicality.

In presenting Bakhtin's ideas I have begun with utterance and voice, in order to explicate them in ways that would be most readily interpretable from the perspective of contemporary Western paradigms of language, speech, and communication. From Bakhtin's perspective, however, the explication should begin with dialogicality. Bakhtin's concern with dialogicality surfaces everywhere in his writings. As he says, "the utterance is filled with *dialogic overtones*" (1986, p. 102). It recurs in particular throughout his translinguistic analyses; indeed, as he also notes, "dialogic relationships . . . are the subject of metalinguistics" (1981, p. 182). His claims about the role of the counter word in understanding reflect this assumption: "To understand another person's utterance means to orient oneself with respect to it, to find the proper place for it in the corresponding context. For each word of the utterance that we are in process of understanding, we, as it were, lay down a set of our own answering words. The greater their number and weight, the deeper and more substantial our understanding will be . . . *Any true understanding is dialogic in nature*. Understanding is to utterance as one line of a dialogue is to the next" (Voloshinov, 1973, p. 102).

By examining the principles of dialogicality, Bakhtin was able to explore several other major issues: the relation between the voices of author and hero in novelistic discourse (Bakhtin, 1981), the nature of interaction between analyst and analysand in psychoanalysis (Voloshinov, 1988), and the history of voices in reported speech (Voloshinov, 1973).

The category of dialogicality is very general. In Bakhtin's view the "primordial dialogism of discourse" (1981, p. 275) is to be found in the ways in which one speaker's concrete utterances come into contact with, or "interanimate," the utterances of another. One form of such "dialogic interanimation" is "direct, face-to-face, vocalized verbal communication between persons" (Voloshinov, 1973, p. 95). This is the form of communicative activity that typically comes to mind when one thinks of dialogue, and it played a fundamental role in much of Bakhtin's thinking. As I have noted, it underlies his account of understanding, and it surfaced in his examination of inner speech (which, as for Vygotsky, derives from social processes). In this latter connection, he asserted that "the units of which inner speech is constituted are certain *whole entities* somewhat resembling a passage of monologic speech or whole utterances. But most of all, they resemble the *alternating lines of a dialogue*. There was good reason why thinkers in ancient times should have conceived of inner speech as *inner dialogue*" (Voloshinov, 1973, p. 38). The nature of face-to-face dialogicality was under investigation by several scholars at the time *Marxism and the Philosophy of Language* (Voloshinov, 1973) was published in 1929. The works of theorists such as L. P. Yakubinskii (1923) were particularly important. They focused on how processes such as abbreviation occur in social speech (and here, Vygotsky also derived many of his ideas about abbreviation in egocentric and inner speech). In all these cases the emphasis was on the ways in which one concrete voice and set of utterances could come into contact with others.

Bakhtin was also concerned with other ways in which an individual speaker's utterances can take on a dialogic orientation toward the utterances of others. One form of such dialogic orientation is parody, a process in which one voice transmits what another voice has said but does so with a "shift in accent" (Bakhtin, 1984, p. 199). This is a dialogic, or multivoiced, phenomenon because the overtones of irony and sarcasm that emerge in parody are due to the simultaneous presence of both the transmitting and the transmitted voices. Parody is a process that can be used to illustrate a wide range of Bakhtin's claims about utterance, voice, and dialogicality.

As an example of how all these constructs come into play, let us consider the parodic uses of a well-known utterance from American political discourse. The utterance occurred in the context of the events surrounding the Watergate scandal in 1973, which brought down Richard M. Nixon's presidency. During the early stages of the affair, Nixon's press secretary, Ronald L. Ziegler, issued many statements about the case, most of which amounted to denials of wrongdoing by Nixon and his associates. As more facts were revealed in judicial proceedings and hearings in the U.S. Senate, however, it became more and more obvious that Ziegler's statements had been false. On April 17, 1973, after some particularly embarrassing disclosures had emerged through other sources, Ziegler termed all previous White House statements on the case "inoperative."

Inoperative is an otherwise normal English word that can be used in a variety of contexts. But once Ziegler had used it in the highly visible, tense debate over an American president's conduct, it took on a different meaning. It became a term that people familiar with that context could no longer use in a neutral way. For those who had experienced that context, "inoperative" became a term strongly associated with a particular socioculturally situated voice, and hence, one that would always be connected with that voice. If parents were to say to their children after April 17, 1973, that the previous statements they had made about rules for going to bed were now "inoperative," it could be taken by many to be a parody of Ziegler's statement and thus an attempt at humor, a sign of resignation to the course of events, and so forth.

From a Bakhtinian perspective, parodies on Ziegler's use of "inoperative" provide a clear illustration of the usefulness of the constructs of utterance, voice, and dialogicality. In this view, utterances always *belong* to someone (that is, a voice). This speaking consciousness may be so visible it is impossible for others to use a term like "inoperative" without recognizing the history of its ownership. In contrast to this Bakhtinian translinguistic approach, linguistic analyses that treat utterances as if they "belong to nobody" (1986, p. 99) cannot capture this essential dimension of meaning. In Bakhtin's analysis, the effects of parody derive directly from the fact that any utterance is "filled with *dialogic overtones*" (1986, p. 102). In using the term "inoperative," many speakers hear both the voice of Ronald Ziegler and their own producing the concrete utterance.

Social Languages

In general, the primordial dialogism of discourse involves a "dialogic orientation" of the utterances of one person to the utterances of others "inside a *single* language." This contrasts with two other fundamental forms of dialogic orientation Bakhtin envisioned: the dialogic orientation among 'social languages' within a single *national* language" and the dialogic orientation among "different national languages within the same *culture*" (1981, p. 275). In order to understand what Bakhtin had in mind in dealing with these two types of dialogue, we must look at his notion of *language*.

By switching from dealing with utterances to dealing with languages, Bakhtin was moving from unique speech events (individual utterances produced by unique voices) to categories or *types* of speech events (types of utterances produced by types of voices). Since "the utterance itself is individual and unreproducible" (Voloshinov, 1973, p. 199), any concern with types of speech events, as in the study of languages, may at first appear to fall outside the boundaries of translinguistics. This is not so, however, because unlike analyses that focus on linguistic objects abstracted from all aspects of the speech event (including voice), Bakhtin's account of languages retains the notion of voice as well as dialogicality. Furthermore, he was also concerned with the struggle between system and performance that is played out in the utterance. Because utterances and voices (now considered as types) are still viewed as two sides of the same coin and dialogicality is still at the center of attention, the analysis of "languages" does indeed fall within the realm of translinguistics.

Bakhtin's notion of national language is that of "the traditional linguistic unities (English, Russian, French, etc.) with their coherent grammatical and semantic systems" (Holquist and Emerson, 1981, p. 430). In reality, however, as Clark and Holquist (1984) point out, the notion of a unitary national language is an "academic fiction" that papers over the effects of centrifugal forces that seek to stratify and change it (p. 13). What Bakhtin had in mind in talking about dialogic orientation among national languages are the ways in which various languages in a cultural setting are employed: one national language may be used at home, another in formal instructional settings, and yet a third in religious ceremonies.

Bakhtin's concern goes beyond this, however, because for him it was not simply a matter of distribution in the use of various national languages; it was also a matter of how these languages and their uses are interrelated or enter into dialogic interanimation (how one language, for example, may be used to provide counter words to another). This is the kind of phenomenon often studied under the heading of "code switching" in contemporary sociolinguistics (Gumperz, 1983). Bakhtin provided relatively little concrete detail on how national languages might enter into dialogic contact. In connection with "social languages," however, he was more specific.

For Bakhtin, a social language is "a discourse peculiar to a specific stratum of society (professional, age group, etc.) within a given social system at a given time" (Holquist and Emerson, 1981, p. 430). Throughout his writing Bakhtin used a variety of terms to refer to social languages. Sometimes he spoke of "social speech types" and in many places he simply used the term "language." I shall employ the term "social language" in what follows, the term "social" serving to distinguish a social language from a national language.

Any national language can be used in connection with several social languages, and a social language can invoke more than one national language. Hence, national languages and social languages can, at least to some extent, be considered independent of one another. As examples of social languages, or social speech types, Bakhtin mentioned "social dialects, characteristic group behavior, professional jargons, generic languages, languages of generations and age groups, tendentious languages, languages of the authorities of various circles and of passing fashions, languages that serve the specific sociopolitical purposes of the day" (1981, p. 262).

Bakhtin's way of defining and analyzing social language allowed him to see order where linguists have traditionally seen only randomness. Following the lead of Ferdinand de Saussure (1959), many twentieth-century linguists have argued that such randomness falls within the scientifically uninvestigable realm of *parole*. Instead of trying to examine these realms, these scholars have opted to focus on those areas of language that result from abstracting the linguistic code from concrete speech activity, including the speaking voice. This has given rise to a focus in much of linguistics on *langue*. As Holquist (1986) has noted, Bakhtin was able to carry out studies of actual human communication because he was not constrained by the restrictions that follow from accepting the Saussurian distinction between *langue* and *parole:* " 'Communication' as Bakhtin uses the term does indeed cover many of the aspects of Saussure's *parole,* for it is concerned with what happens when real people in all the contingency of their myriad lives actually speak to each other. But Saussure conceived the individual language user to be an absolutely free agent with the ability to choose any words to implement a particular intention. Saussure concluded, not surprisingly, that language as used by heterogeneous millions of such willful subjects was unstudiable, a chaotic jungle beyond the capacity of science to domesticate" (p. xvi).

Rather than view voices and utterances in such chaotic terms, Bakhtin was able to find patterns of organization that derive from the notion of social languages. He "begins by assuming that individual speakers do not have the kind of freedom *parole* assumes they have" (Holquist, 1986, p. xvi). As Bakhtin wrote, "the single utterance, with all its individuality and creativity, can in no way be regarded as a *completely free combination* of forms of language, as is supposed, for example, by Saussure (and by many other linguists after him), who juxtaposed the utterance (*la parole*), as a purely individual act, to the system of language as a phenomenon that is purely social and mandatory for the individuum" (Bakhtin, 1986, p. 81). By employing the notion of social language, then, Bakhtin was able to identify and study the organizing principles of concrete speech communication. His effort was grounded in the assumption that one does not have to examine units that "belong to nobody and are addressed to nobody" in order to formulate principles of human communication that generalize across utterances.

In Bakhtin's view, a speaker always invokes a social language in producing an utterance, and this social language shapes what the speaker's individual voice can say. This process of producing unique utterances by speaking in social languages involves a specific kind of dialogicality or multivoicedness that Bakhtin termed "ventriloquation" (Bakhtin, 1981; Holquist, 1981), the process whereby one voice speaks *through* another voice or voice type in a social language: "The word in language is half someone else's. It becomes 'one's own' only when the speaker populates it with his own intention, his own accent, when he appropriates the word, adapting it to his own semantic and expressive intention. Prior to this moment of appropriation, the word does not exist in a neutral and impersonal language (it is not, after all, out of a dictionary that the speaker gets his words!), but rather it exists in other people's mouths, in other people's concrete contexts, serving other people's intentions: it is from there that one must take the word, and make it one's own" (Bakhtin, 1981, pp. 293–294).

As an example of how Bakhtin harnessed the notions of voice, dialogicality (including ventriloquism), and social language in his concrete analyses, let us consider what he termed the "hybrid construction." A hybrid construction is "an utterance that belongs, by its grammatical (syntactic) and compositional markers, to a single speaker, but that actually contains mixed within it two utterances, two speech manners, two styles, two 'languages', two semantic and axiological belief systems" (pp. 304–305).* He developed this notion in the course of his examination of the organizing principles that govern the narrator's voice in English comic novels. In this connection, he analyzed the following passage from Dickens's *Little Dorrit*:

> That illustrious man and great national ornament, Mr. Merdle, continued his shining course. It began to be widely understood that one who had done society the admirable service *of making so much money out of it,* could not be suffered to remain a commoner. A baronetcy was spoken of with confidence; a peerage was frequently mentioned. (italics in original; p. 306)

---

*As Emerson (1989) notes, the term "conceptual horizon" may be more appropriate than "belief system" for *krugozor,* the Russian word used by Bakhtin.

As Bakhtin notes, in the first sentence of this passage the narrator uses the "concealed speech of another," namely the "hypocritically ceremonial general opinion of Merdle." Indeed, in the text preceding the italicized phrase the narrator is ventriloquating through this social language. When it comes to the italicized segment, however, we hear "the words of the author himself (as if put in parentheses in the quotation)." Two distinct social languages have thus been appropriated in the creation of this passage. The lack of any obvious surface marking of the boundary between the two social languages invoked makes this a hybrid construction, in which, in Bakhtin's description, "the subordinate clause is in direct authorial speech and the main clause in someone else's speech. The main and subordinate clauses are constructed in different semantic and axiological conceptual systems [different social languages]" (p. 306). In addition to the dialogicality produced through ventriloquism in the Dickens excerpt, a second form arises from the juxtaposition of the two voices in a seemingly continuous flow of text. It is this juxtaposition of utterances in the chain of speech communication that gives rise to the sardonic effect of the passage: the utterances of the two voices "are not self-sufficient; they are aware of and mutually reflect one another" (Bakhtin, 1986, p. 91).

Speech Genres

In his account of the hybrid construction (and elsewhere) Bakhtin dealt with social languages that have no particularly obvious or regular overt markers attached to them. There is nothing in the form, such as the appearance of a different dialect or vocabulary, or the use of unique tense and aspect forms, that distinguishes one social language from another. In considering other social speech types, however, Bakhtin posited the existence of clear surface marking. This he spelled out in most detail in connection with his ideas about "generic languages" or "speech genres."

Bakhtin recognized that the study of such genres was in its infancy, noting that "no list of oral speech genres yet exists, or even a principle on which such a list might be based" (1986, p. 80). He did, however, occasionally provide sample lists of the kind of phenomena he had in mind, which included military commands; everyday genres of greeting, farewell, and congratulation; salon conversations about everyday, social, aesthetic, and other subjects; genres of table conversation; intimate conversations among friends; and everyday narration. According to Bakhtin, "a speech genre is not a form of language, but a typical form [a type] of utterance; as such the genre also includes a certain typical kind of expression that inheres in it. In the genre the word acquires a particular typical expression. Genres correspond to typical situations of speech communication, typical themes, and, consequently, also to particular contacts between the *meanings* of words and actual concrete reality under certain typical circumstances" (Bakhtin, 1986, p. 87). In contrast to social languages, where the distinguishing feature is the social stratum of the speakers, speech genres are characterized primarily in terms of the "typical situations of speech communication." The two phenomena and the two sets of criteria may be viewed as analytically distinct, but in reality they are often thoroughly intertwined: speakers from certain social strata (for example, the military) are the ones who invoke the speech genre of military commands.

In Bakhtin's view, the production of any utterance entails the invocation of a speech genre: "We speak only in definite speech genres, that is, all our utterances have definite and relatively stable typical *forms of construction of the whole*. Our repertoire of oral (and written) speech genres is rich. We use them confidently and skillfully *in practice*, and it is quite possible for us not even to suspect their existence *in theory*. Like Molière's Monsieur Jourdain who, when speaking in prose, had no idea that was what he was doing, we speak in diverse genres without suspecting that they exist" (1986, p. 78). Thus, in Bakhtin's view it is no more possible to produce an utterance without using some speech genre than it is possible to produce an utterance without using some national language, such as English.

Quite independently (at least until very recently) several scholars in anthropology, the ethnography of speaking, and sociolinguistics have developed their own ideas about speech genres, which can help clarify Bakhtin's. Richard Bauman and colleagues (1987) note that for ethnographers of speaking, "genre . . . has generally been understood as a conventionalized utterance type, a ready-made way of packaging speech . . . [One should understand] genre as a resource for performance, available to speakers for the realization of specific social ends in a variety of creative, emergent, and even unique ways" (pp. 5–6). This description is consistent with the criterion of multivoicedness Bakhtin used in defining speech genres. In particular, the fact that genre is a "ready-made way of packaging speech" that at the same time allows for "creative, emergent, and even unique" individual performances means that both the voice type of a speech genre and a concrete individual voice are simultaneously involved. In Bakhtin's terminology, the latter "populates" or "appropriates" the former.

Another ethnographer of speaking, Susan Philips, lists two additional characteristics of the notion of a speech genre: "First, [speech genres] are often named or lexicalized forms of speech within the [national] language used by members of the cultures studied, so that the claim that they exist as distinct forms of speech in the minds of the people being studied can be warranted. Examples of such in English include speeches, stories, songs, and prayers. Second, the speech which constitutes them is typically routinized and predictable, and also contiguous and bounded by framing devices. These qualities allow the researchers to determine when they begin and end, so that a naturally occurring unit of activity for study may be identified" (1987, p. 26). When Bakhtin provided sample lists of speech genres, the lists he made were of "named or lexicalized forms of speech." He would therefore seem to be in agreement with Philips in his focus on this property. But his claim that it is possible to use speech genres *in practice* while not suspecting their existence *in theory* would seem to reflect a certain ambivalence on this matter. This is so because the "theory" involved is tied to conscious reflection, and as Michael Silverstein (1987) has noted, for speakers a major determinant of the process of conscious reflection is lexicalization. Thus, whereas ethnographers of speaking sometimes stress accessibility to conscious awareness in defining speech genres, Bakhtin seemed to be content to assume that such genres often exist in practice only and must be explicated through translinguistic analysis.

Philips's second set of criteria (routinization, predictability, contiguity, and the presence of framing devices) is generally consistent with Bakhtin's notion of speech genre. In his view, "when hearing others' speech, we guess its genre from the very first words; we predict a certain length (that is, the approximate length of the speech whole) and a certain compositional structure; we foresee the end" (1986, p. 79).

In some respects the recent work of ethnographers of speaking goes beyond the specification of speech genres Bakhtin provided. Their notion of framing devices is an important addition. The main point at which the ideas of ethnographers of speaking, such as Bauman and Philips, differ from Bakhtin's is in the latter's explicit focus on the category of dialogicality. The phenomenon of ventriloquation, and the fact that one of the defining features of a speech genre is the addressivity it involves, distinguishes his ideas from theirs. Just as in other areas, dialogicality is the notion that makes this aspect of his thinking unique.

An Illustration

A shorthand way of formulating Bakhtin's ideas about dialogicality for a sociocultural approach to mind is to pose a fundamental Bakhtinian question about forms of semiotic mediation: "Who is doing the talking?" From a Bakhtinian perspective, the answer will always be: "At least two voices." His account of social languages and speech genres means that, in addition to the concrete speaking consciousness producing the unique utterance, a voice type must also be involved. At the same time, his various comments about the primordial dialogue of discourse indicate that other concrete speaking consciousnesses might be involved as well.

To illustrate the importance of this general Bakhtinian question and how some of Bakhtin's more specific constructs fit into the picture, I shall turn to an example from a peculiar form of discourse in the sociocultural context of modern American political life: presidential campaign speeches. Specifically, I shall draw on George Bush's speech accepting the Republican nomination for president, which he made at the Republican National Convention in the summer of 1988. In the passage I want to discuss, Bush said:

> We've created 17 million new jobs in the past five years, more than twice as many as Europe and Japan combined. And they're good jobs. The majority of them created in the past six years paid an average of more than $22,000 a year. Someone better take "a message to Michael": tell him we've been creating good jobs at good wages. The fact is, they talk, we deliver. They promise, we perform. (*New York Times*, August 19, 1988, p. A14)

From the standpoint of American political rhetoric, there is nothing particularly unusual about this passage. It did not break any new ground nor did it break Bush's promise to "hold my charisma in check." The passage is interesting, however, as an object of Bakhtinian translinguistic analysis. Its explication reveals dialogic processes involving internal as well as external speech and dialogic processes between unique voices as well as between social languages.

If one poses the Bakhtinian question "Who is doing the talking?," in this case, a first, superficial answer might be George Bush. But a moment's consideration reveals several ways in which other voices are involved in the production of these utterances. At least two of these are generally true of most modern campaign speeches by presidential candidates.

First, in making such speeches, concrete individual voices ventriloquate through a particular speech genre. The stylization involved in "The fact is, they talk, we deliver. They promise, we perform" reflects the "definite and relatively stable typical forms of construction of the whole" Bakhtin spoke of in discussing speech genres. Second, modern presidential campaign speeches are the product of several hands. An initial draft may contain passages by different speech writers, and these may in turn be reworked by other writers and by the candidate before they are presented. The end product is one in which the informed ear can hear a polyphony of voices.

At the same time, there are several points of dialogicality specific to Bush's speech. Let us consider first an aspect of the speech that relies on a dialogic encounter between unique voices. The unique voices here were those of Bush and the presidential candidate of the Democratic Party, Michael Dukakis. The specific kind of dialogic encounter involved is parody, a process whose effect derives from a type of ventriloquation.

In the passage from Bush's speech quoted above, the comment "tell him we've been creating good jobs at good wages" involves this kind of ventriloquation. In the 1988 campaign Michael Dukakis constantly mentioned the need to create "good jobs at good wages." This refrain was motivated by the Democrats' claim that even though new jobs had been created during the Reagan administration, many of them were temporary, low paying, and lacking in fringe benefits. The strategy Bush and his speech writers used to challenge this claim was to appropriate Dukakis's words rather than object to them overtly. The parodic effect they sought derived from the simultaneous presence of Bush's and Dukakis's voices.

Additional kinds of dialogicality become apparent in considering the relationship of Bush's utterances to other utterances and voices. The process through which the audience understood his speech involved a dialogic encounter between his utterances and their utterances (overt or covert). At first glance the heavy emphasis on the role of listener response in Bakhtin's account of understanding would seem to indicate that this process could generate as many interpretations as there are listeners. At a political convention of three thousand, his account suggests that a speaker's utterances could be understood in three thousand different ways because three thousand distinct voices are interacting with these utterances. Of course this is not to mention the audience created by the media. It is as if each listener wished to raise his or her hand and say, "Yes, but what about X?" where X could be different in each case.

This kind of diversity, however, is constrained by the social languages invoked by the audience as they listened to Bush's speech. The functioning of social languages is particularly in evidence in the process listeners used to understand Bush's statement, "Someone better take 'a message to Michael.' " This phrase comes directly from a 1966 pop music song by Dionne Warwick entitled "Take a Message to Michael," which Bush appropriated specifically to appeal to younger voters. This appeal was a major part of his campaign and was reflected in his selection of the youthful J. Danforth Quayle as his vice-presidential running mate. Michael Oreskes, a *New York Times* writer, touched on Bush's rhetorical strategy in his article, "Bush's Gamble: Republican Ticket Hopes to Bridge More than One Gap." In the article, devoted largely to Bush's attempt to obtain the support of women and younger people for the Republican ticket, Oreskes wrote: "Mr. Bush's effort to combine conservative and generational appeal was underscored in his acceptance speech Thursday night. He summarized his readiness to fight for conservative principles by urging that someone 'take a message to Michael.' Older voters may have heard only a shot at the Democratic nominee. But younger voters recognized the refrain of a popular late 1960's love song" ("Week in Review," August 19, 1988).

In Bakhtinian terms, the rhetorical strategy employed by Bush and his speech writers in their use of the expression "take a message to Michael" involves several forms of dialogicality. First, by appropriating the words of a speech genre (1960s pop music) and a song by a particular pop artist, Bush created an utterance in which more than one voice was speaking. Second, from the listeners' perspective ventriloquation was involved, because in the process of coming into dialogic contact with Bush's utterance, the inner speech utterances of the members of the audience may themselves have been shaped by the speech genre of pop music. This dialogic encounter undoubtedly varied for listeners from different generations, that is, listeners with different repertoires of social languages. Thus, as Oreskes notes, older voters "may have heard only a shot at the Democratic nominee," whereas younger voters also heard something else, namely Bush's appeal for solidarity with them. Different "[social] languages of generations and age groups" (Bakhtin, 1981, p. 262) shaped the inner speech responses and hence, the understanding, of different segments of Bush's audience.

There are obviously a host of other issues one could raise in analyzing a passage such as this from a Bakhtinian perspective. But my purpose is not to provide a full interpretation of Bush's speech; rather, it is to illustrate the kinds of issues illuminated by this perspective. They are issues that have a great deal to say about the nature of meaning and thus about the processes and prospects of semiotic mediation. The major point I want to make is that Bakhtin's approach to semiotic phenomena continually emphasizes the notion that utterances and utterance meaning are inherently situated in sociocultural context. Because the production of any utterance involves the appropriation of at least one social language and speech genre, and because these social speech types are socioculturally situated, the ensuing account assumes that meaning is inextricably linked with historical, cultural, and institutional setting.

4

The Multivoicedness of Meaning

Bakhtin's ideas, as I suggested in Chapter 3, have major implications for a Vygotskian approach to mediated action. In this chapter I shall expand on some of these implications as they relate to the issue of meaning. A Bakhtinian orientation to meaning leads down paths not often traveled in social science analyses, paths that explore voices, social languages, speech genres, and dialogicality.

Meaning is central to the sociocultural approach to mediated action I have outlined precisely because the notion of mediation is central. The processes and structures of semiotic mediation provide a crucial link between historical, cultural, and institutional contexts on the one hand and the mental functioning of the individual on the other. Of course, this does not mean that a semiotic orientation can automatically be equated with a focus on meaning. Many semiotic analyses concern themselves primarily with the issues of formal structure that are at the center of much of contemporary linguistics.

Yet this was not the direction Vygotsky and Bakhtin took. Following in a longstanding Russian tradition grounded in the "priority of semantics" (Clark and Holquist, 1984, p. 11), they focused on ways in which language and other semiotic systems could be used to produce meaning, especially meaning as it shapes human action.

A motivating force behind the priority Bakhtin gave to semantics and a force closely tied to the fundamental Bakhtinian question "Who is doing the talking?" can be formulated in terms of "Who owns meaning?" (Holquist, 1981). As Holquist has noted, views range from the claim that no one owns meaning—for example, Deconstructionists' claim that the "human voice is conceived merely as another means for registering differences"—to the claim that particular individuals own meaning. Proponents of the former position have criticized those of the latter on the basis of the argument that "the very conception of meaning, to say nothing of persons, invoked in most traditional episte-mologies begins by illicitly assuming a presence whose end Nietzsche really was announcing when he let it be known that God had died in history" (pp. 164–165).

In Bakhtin's approach, we find an underlying claim that in some ways appears to be an intermediate one between the position that individuals own meaning and the position that no one owns meaning. But because it is grounded in processes of dialogicality it is not some kind of unprincipled compromise and, indeed, differs from both these positions in productive ways. In Bakhtin's view, users of language "rent" meaning (Holquist, 1981, p. 164). In other words, "I can mean what I say, but only *indirectly*, at a second remove, in the words I take and give back to the community according to the protocols it establishes. My voice can mean, but only with others: at times in chorus, but at the best of times in a dialogue" (p. 165).

This renting metaphor is, of course, another form of the claim that the answer to the Bakhtinian question "Who is doing the talking?" always involves at least two voices. It is a metaphor that emerged more naturally and was more readily accepted in the sociocultural setting in which Bakhtin worked, which did not stress the individualism and atomism characteristic of the modern West. Instead of seeking the source of meaning production in the isolated individual, it follows the more collectivist orientation of Russian culture and assumes that meaning is always based in group life.

Holquist's metaphor is quite useful when it comes to specifying some of the concrete ways in which Bakhtin's theory of meaning is distinct from other theories that guide the thinking of western schol-ars, especially those raised in the Anglo-American tradition. I shall address these differences by mapping out four issues, all of which can be formulated as aspects of a Bakhtinian approach to meaning. These are 1) rejection of a "disengaged image of the self" and the "atomism" associated with it; 2) recognition of a "dialogic" as well as a "univocal" text function; 3) recognition of the authority attached to a text; and 4) rejection of literal meaning as the starting point for a theory of meaning.

Rejection of a "Disengaged Image of the Self"

My claims about the "disengaged image of the self" stem primarily from the writings of Charles Taylor (1985a, 1985b, 1989). Taylor has been struck by the tenacity with which western scholars hold to the underlying assumptions of approaches such as behaviorism, in spite of what he sees as overwhelming evidence that these assumptions lead to untenable claims. Taylor ties the emergence of what he terms the disengaged image of the self to the major cosmological shift that occurred in the West in the seventeeth century, which was marked by a transition from viewing the world order in terms of ideas to viewing it in terms of mechanism. The resulting disengaged image of the self is part of a "typically modern notion of freedom as the ability to act on one's own, without outside interference or subordination to outside authority" (1985a, p. 5).

Taylor argues that in addition to the "understandable prestige of the natural science model," the assumptions that underlie the disengaged image of the self spring from certain fundamental beliefs characteristic of our sociocultural and historical context. In particular, he argues that "behind and supporting the impetus to naturalism . . . stands an attachment to a certain picture of the agent." This picture holds great attraction for us; it is "both flattering and inspiring [because] it shows us as capable of achieving a kind of disengagement from our world by objectifying it" (p. 4).

In Taylor's view, one of the most noteworthy (and detrimental) consequences of the disengaged image of the self is "atomism." The concept of atomism he has in mind is tied to an understanding of the individual as "metaphysically independent of society." Contemporary atomistic views clearly allow for processes whereby individuals are shaped by their social environment; indeed, as Taylor notes, "the early atomism of the seventeenth century seems incredible to us." What atomism "hides from view is the way in which an individual is constituted by language and culture which can only be maintained and renewed in the communities he is part of" (1985a, p. 8).

Taylor has specific issues in mind when he writes of how an individual is constituted by language, and these are not always the same issues raised by Bakhtin. What these two thinkers have in common is their rejection of the idea that individuals are "metaphysically independent of society," a point that is played out in Bakhtin's approach in relation to the question "Who is doing the talking?" As noted in Chapter 3, Bakhtin rejected the notion that isolated individuals create utterances and meaning. This rejection is implicit throughout his account of dialogicality, and scholars such as Holquist (1986) have made it quite explicit when comparing Bakhtin's account with Saussure's assumptions about *parole*. This does not mean that the speaker or writer must be or can be totally subordinated to outside authority; to do so would be to revert to a kind of monologism that Bakhtin criticized in his account of the "authoritative word." What it does mean is that for Bakhtin, a kind of "interference" and "subordination" is an inherent part of any utterance and its meaning, a fact that ultimately follows from the general observation that an utterance is always a link in the chain of speech communication.

In a Bakhtinian approach, interference and subordination come in many forms, but they are especially evident in the process of ventriloquation. The notion of ventriloquation presupposes that a voice is never solely responsible for creating an utterance or its meaning. It begins with the fact that "the word in language is half someone else's." (Bakhtin, 1981, pp. 293–294). In a view grounded in ventriloquation, then, the very act of speaking precludes any claims about the individual's being "metaphysically independent of society" (Taylor, 1985a, p. 8).

Among other things, Taylor's comments on the idea of the disengaged image of the self and on atomism are useful because they highlight the fact that problems in understanding a position such as Bakhtin's reflect the general sociocultural situatedness of those doing the understanding. Taylor reminds us that assumptions such as those underlying atomism are natural for modern western scholars because they are consistent with the pervasive, everyday assumptions in our sociocultural setting. In this view the image of the disengaged self is not created or manifested only in psychology or other social sciences. It "is woven into a host of modern practices—economic, scientific, technological, psychotherapeutic, and so on" (p. 5). Indeed, one of Taylor's major points is that, despite their lack of intellectual or scientific merit, atomistic positions continue to appeal to us in the West because they are consistent with underlying, historically specific cultural assumptions.

If this claim is correct, one can expect the same kind of resistance to perspectives such as Bakhtin's that Taylor has noted in other cases. And even when there is an explicit desire to accept such a perspective, one can expect this alternative position to be recast in subtle and not-so-subtle ways as it is assimilated into existing theoretical and cultural worldviews. Such tendencies highlight the fact that understanding and assimilating new theoretical ideas may have as much to do with the sociocultural background of the investigators as with the theoretical perspective these investigators overtly espouse.

The Univocal and Dialogic Functions of Texts

During the past few decades, a particular view of human communication has come to dominate much of the research in developmental psychology and other social sciences. According to this view, human communication can be conceptualized in terms of the *transmission* of information. This transmission model involves the translation (or "encoding") of an idea into a signal by a sender, the transmission of this signal to a receiver, and the "decoding" of the signal into a message by the receiver.

The origins of this approach can be traced to several sources. Per Linell (1988) notes precursors extending back at least to Locke (see also Parkinson, 1977; Harris, 1981). It is now generally recognized that in more recent times a major impetus for this model came from C. E. Shannon and Warren Weaver's (1949) mathematical information theory. Yet a close reading of their original theoretical statements reveals that their ideas cannot be equated to a simple transmission model. As theorists such as Michael Reddy (1979) have noted, however, the definition of information and communication that emerged from mathematical information theory soon came to be transformed through the influence of widely used metaphors (an aspect of scholars' mediational means) that shape our thinking and speaking about communication. These metaphors can be considered another major source (indeed, *the* major source if Reddy is right) of contemporary views about the transmission model of communication.

Reddy reviewed a wide range of metaphors concerned with communication in English, of which the following are a sample:

(1) Try to get your thought across better.
(2) Whenever you have a good idea practice capturing it in words.
(3) Can you actually extract coherent ideas from that prose?

On the basis of his analysis, he outlined the underlying "conduit metaphor" that seems to shape a great deal of our understanding of human communication. The basic outlines of the conduit metaphor, at least in its "major framework" version, consist of the following points: "1) language functions like a conduit, transferring thoughts bodily from one person to another; 2) in writing and speaking, people insert their thoughts or feelings in the words; 3) words accomplish the transfer by containing the thoughts or feelings and conveying them to others; and 4) in listening or reading, people extract the thoughts and feelings once again from the words" (p. 290).

Reddy does not claim that the conduit metaphor makes it impossible to think about communication in other ways. Indeed, he views mathematical information theory as an example of how viable alternatives have been formulated and outlines one of his own. In his view, however, thinking about communication that avoids the conduit metaphor tends to "remain brief, isolated, and fragmentary in the face of an entrenched system of opposing attitudes and assumptions" (pp. 297–298). The metaphors about communication in English are so heavily weighted in favor of conduit notions that "practically speaking, if you try to avoid all obvious conduit metaphor expressions in your usage, you are nearly struck dumb when communication becomes the topic" (p. 299). According to Reddy, the power of this basic metaphor is largely responsible for the misinterpretation of information theory, even by its founders. Because "English has a preferred framework for conceptualizing communication," it ends up being "its own worst enemy" (pp. 285, 286) in this respect.

The transmission model of communication that springs from the conduit metaphor is often represented schematically as in the accompanying diagram.

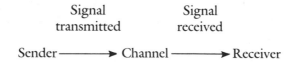

One of the most common criticisms of the transmission model as schematized here concerns the unidirectionality of the arrows involved. Because they are unidirectional, the receiver is viewed as passive (note the very term *receiver*). As Reddy points out, "in the framework of the conduit metaphor, the listener's task must be one of extraction. He must find the meaning 'in the words' and take it out of them, so that it 'gets into his head' " (p. 288). Because the receiver's task is viewed as being simply one of extraction, "to the extent that the conduit metaphor does see communication as requiring some slight expenditure of energy, it localizes this expenditure almost totally in the speaker or writer. The function of the reader or listener is trivialized" (p. 308).

From a Bakhtinian perspective the schematization of the transmission model is problematic above all due to the inherently monologic assumptions that underlie it. These assumptions, reflected, among other places, in the schema's unidirectional arrows, run counter to Bakhtin's idea that understanding involves one voice's response to another, a process in which "for each word of the utterance that we are in process of understanding, we, as it were, lay down a set of our answering words" (Voloshinov, 1973, p. 102).

Furthermore, from a Bakhtinian perspective also, the assumption that it is possible to speak of a single, unaltered meaning or message is problematic. Again, instead of two voices coming into contact and interanimating one another, the communication model schematized above (at least as interpreted in terms of the conduit metaphor) assumes that the sender encodes, or packages, a single meaning and transmits it to the receiver, who passively decodes or fails to decode it. The "it" remains the same throughout. Finally, instead of viewing senders as being influenced by past and future receivers, as a Bakhtinian approach suggests, models such as that sketched out above treat messages as if they can be understood outside the extended flow of speech communication.

The basic contradictions I have noted between a Bakhtinian and a transmission approach to communication can be resolved in one of two ways. First, it could be argued that one approach is correct and the other is incorrect. The problem with this is that both the transmission model (even as distorted by the metaphor structure of English) and a Bakhtinian approach have yielded important insights into communication processes. A second course would be to identify some way in which the insights of the two approaches can be incorporated into a more inclusive framework. This does not mean that some kind of unmotivated combination should be created, a compromise that would dilute the insights of both approaches. Instead, this framework could be based on a claim that utterances or texts can function *in more than one way*. Such a claim has been outlined by Yuri Lotman (1988b), who assumes a "functional dualism of texts in a cultural system." The two basic functions he sees texts fulfilling are "to convey meanings adequately, and to generate new meanings" (p. 34). The first of these is very similar to the function presupposed by the transmission model of communication: "The first function is fulfilled best when the codes of the speaker and the listener most completely coincide and, consequently, when the text has the maximum degree of univocality. The ideal boundary mechanism for such an operation would be an artificial language and a text in an artificial language. The gravitation toward standardization, which generates artificial languages, and the tendency toward self-description, which creates metalinguistic constructions, are not external to the linguistic and cultural mechanism" (p. 34).

As Lotman notes, this text function has been at the core of language study. One reason is that "it is this aspect of a text that is most easily modeled with the means at our disposal." The "means" involved here are of course the mediational means that appear in the form of theories used by linguists, communication scientists, and others. The overwhelming tendency to presuppose the univocal function in these approaches has resulted in a situation in which this function has "at times . . . been identified with a text as such, obfuscating the other aspects" (p. 35).

In contrast to this first, transmissionlike function of a text, the second is grounded in the kind of multivoicedness that so concerned Bakhtin. I shall term it the "dialogic" function to contrast it with the univocality Lotman associates with the first function: "The second function of text is to generate new meanings. In this respect a text ceases to be a passive link in conveying some constant information between input (sender) and output (receiver). Whereas in the first case a difference between the message at the input and that at the output of an information circuit can occur only as a result of a defect in the communications channel, and is to be attributed to the technical imperfections of this system, in the second case such a difference is the very essence of a text's function as a 'thinking device.' What from the first standpoint is a defect, from the second is a norm, and vice versa" (pp. 36–37). Lotman argues that this second, dialogic function of text is more interesting than the univocal function for the semiotic study of culture. Instead of focusing on the transmission of meaning it points the way to understanding the generation of meaning, a process that can occur on the intramental as well as the intermental plane of functioning.

In Lotman's view both functions of text can be found in any sociocultural setting, but one or the other dominates in certain areas of activity or in general during certain periods of history. He argues, for example, that "the mechanism of identification, the elimination of differences and the raising of a text to the status of a standard, does not just serve as a principle guaranteeing that a message will be adequately received in a system of communication: no less important is its function of providing a common memory for the group, of transforming it from an unstructured crowd into 'une personne morale,' to use Rousseau's expression. This function is especially important in nonliterate cultures and in cultures with a dominant mythological consciousness, but it tends also to be present to some degree in any culture" (p. 35).

Lotman's account of functional dualism implies that when a text is serving a dialogic function, it cannot be adequately understood in terms of the transmission model of communication. This is so because a transmission model presupposes that a single, univocal message is transmitted from sender to receiver, whereas Lotman and Bakhtin view the process as involving multiple voices from the outset. As noted earlier, for Bakhtin "understanding strives to match the speaker's word with a *counter word*" (Voloshinov, 1973, p. 102).

Furthermore, Bakhtin's insights into the nature of dialogicality imply that a univocal, transmission model cannot be amended in any simple way to deal with this issue. Making the arrows in the above schema bidirectional might seem to begin to address this issue, and it has often been suggested. Since this is usually taken to mean that two unidirectional messages are involved, however, it does little to resolve the underlying problems associated with presuppositions about univocality.

Many of the properties of the dialogic function reflect the fact that "the main structural attribute of a text in this second function is its internal heterogeneity" (Lotman, 1988b, p. 37). The kind of heterogeneity Lotman has in mind is a heterogeneity of social languages or national languages, and it gives rise to an image rich in the interanimation of voices: "In its second function a text is not a passive receptacle, or bearer of some content placed in it from without, but a generator. The essence of the process of generation, however, is not only an evolution but also, to a considerable extent, an interaction between structures. Their interaction in the closed world of a text becomes an active cultural factor as a working semiotic system. A text of this type is always richer than any particular language [i.e., either a social or a national language] and cannot be put together automatically from it.

A text is a semiotic space in which languages interact, interfere, and organize themselves hierarchically" (p. 37). Among other things, the dynamic processes of this semiotic space allow for the production of a continual stream of new interpretations of a text much like those produced as new readers encounter a work of fiction.

The importance of Lotman's distinction between the univocal and dialogic functions of text can be seen in its relevance to several ongoing debates in the social sciences. For example, consider some of the research of Carol Gilligan (1982). In her book, appropriately entitled *In a Different Voice,* Gilligan explores ways in which psychological theory has failed to take into account women's perspectives, or what Bakhtin might have called women's social languages. The result, according to Gilligan, is that women's responses in interview and therapy sessions are often assessed on criteria developed for males. In at least some cases, this has meant that basic assumptions underlying women's responses have not been recognized and that their answers have therefore been ranked as less developed than men's.

Gilligan's critique of Kohlberg's methods of assessing moral judgment is particularly interesting in this connection. In a chapter entitled "Images of Relationship," she examines the answers of two eleven-year-olds named Jake and Amy to interviewers' questions about how to resolve a moral dilemma. The particular dilemma at issue is perhaps the best-known one in Kohlberg's research. In it the subject is presented with a situation in which a man named Heinz is to decide whether or not to steal a drug to save his wife's life. Heinz does not have the money to buy the drug, and he knows that his wife will die if she is not able to get the drug.

Gilligan's argument is grounded in her observation that the two children approach the moral dilemma from fundamentally different perspectives. Jake approaches it in terms of abstract rules and rights, as a "self-contained problem in moral logic," or in his own words as "sort of like a math problem with humans." In contrast, Amy approaches it from the perspective of "a world comprised of relationships rather than of people standing alone, a world that coheres through human connection rather than through systems of rules." Since the Kohlbergian approach to scoring the interviews is motivated by a search for stages in the development of an abstract logic of moral judgment, Jake's answer is recognizable and receives a higher score than Amy's answer, which "seems evasive and unsure," especially when the interviewer follows some of her initial responses with further questions motivated by a concern with systems of rules and rights (pp. 28–29).

For my purposes, the most interesting aspect of Gilligan's account is her analysis of what it is that Amy was doing and how it contrasts with an analysis that notes that Amy did not conduct sustained argument at a certain stage level. On the basis of the dynamics of the interaction between Amy and interviewer, Gilligan states:

> Amy is answering a different question from the one the interviewer thought had been posed. Amy is considering not *whether* Heinz should act in this situation ("*should* Heinz steal the drug?") but rather *how* Heinz should act in response to this awareness of his wife's needs ("Should Heinz *steal* the drug?"). The interviewer takes the mode of action for granted, presuming it to be a matter of fact; Amy assumes the necessity for action and considers what form it should take. In the interviewer's failure to imagine a response not dreamt of in Kohlberg's moral philosophy lies the failure to hear Amy's question and to see the logic in her response, to discern that what appears, from one perspective, to be an evasion of the dilemma signifies in other terms a recognition of the problem and a search for a more adequate solution. (1982, p. 31)

In terms of the constructs outlined above, Amy is treating the interviewer's questions as a dialogic text, whereas the interviewer and the analysts of the text assumed that they constituted a univocal text as envisioned in a transmission model of communication. This approach to Amy's answer views it as "evasive" because it is not a recognizable response to what had been assumed to be a query with a single interpretation. In contrast, Gilligan's argument says that the voice of response and retort Amy brings to the interview is different from that of Jake. From a Bakhtinian perspective, this means that the processes and outcomes of understanding and interpreting the interviewer's utterances are different. Indeed, Gilligan provides a specific account of the counter-questions posed by Jake and Amy ("*Should* Heinz steal the drug?" versus "Should Heinz *steal* the drug?").

Thus, in contrast to a univocal reading of the interviewer's questions, which presupposes that "the codes of the speaker and listener most completely coincide" (Lotman, 1988b, p. 34), Gilligan is arguing that "Amy is answering a different question from the one the interviewer thought had been posed" (p. 31). In Lotman's terms this reflects the fact that she is treating the question as a "thinking device," with which her voice can interact, instead of an unalterable, univocal message.

Gilligan provides enough detail about the interviews to make this point with some specificity. But it is a point that probably underlies the dynamics and outcomes of a wide range of dialogues between experimenter or interviewer and subject. For example, researchers such as Cole and Scribner (1974) have made similar, quite convincing arguments with regard to studies in cross-cultural psychology. Lotman's insights about the functional dualism of texts suggest a new framework for understanding how dialogue in such settings occurs.

Authority and Text

Lotman's ideas about the two functions of text are closely tied to Bakhtin's distinction between "authoritative" and "internally persuasive" discourse. In addition to the univocality and dialogicality associated with Lotman's two functions, Bakhtin characterized the difference in terms of the degree to which one voice has the authority to come into contact with and interanimate another. This notion of authority will turn out to have important implications in an account of meaning that is intended to deal with issues of how intermental and intramental functioning are socioculturally situated.

In Bakhtin's (1981) view, authoritative discourse is based on the assumption that utterances and their meanings are fixed, not modifiable as they come into contact with new voices: "The authoritative word demands that we acknowledge it, that we make it our own; it binds us, quite independent of any power it might have to persuade us internally; we encounter it with its authority fused to it." The "static and dead" meaning structure of authoritative discourse allows no interanimation with other voices. Instead of functioning as a generator of meaning or as a thinking device, an authoritative text "demands our unconditional allegiance," and it allows "no play with its borders, no gradual and flexible transitions, no spontaneously creative stylizing variants on it."

As examples of authoritative texts, Bakhtin cited religious, political, and moral texts as well as "the word of a father, of adults, of teachers, etc." A text of this sort "enters our verbal consciousness as a compact and indivisible mass; one must either totally affirm it, or totally reject it. It is indissolubly fused with its authority—with political power, an institution, a person—and it stands or falls together with that authority. One cannot divide it up—agree with one part, accept but not completely another part, reject utterly a third part" (pp. 342, 343). Throughout his account of authoritative discourse, Bakhtin emphasized its inability to enter into contact with other voices and social languages. It is for this reason that it gives rise to the kinds of univocal text presupposed by transmission models of communication. As Bakhtin noted, "authoritative discourse cannot be represented—it is only transmitted" (p. 344).

In contrast to authoritative discourse, "the internally persuasive word is half-ours and half-someone else's"; it allows dialogic interanimation. Indeed, "its creativity and productiveness consist precisely in the fact that such a word awakens new and independent words, that it organizes masses of our words from within, and does not remain in an isolated and static condition . . . The semantic structure of an internally persuasive discourse is not *finite*, it is *open*; in each of the new contexts that dialogize it, this discourse is able to reveal ever new *ways to mean*" (pp. 345–346).

For the purposes of developing a sociocultural approach to mediated action, the major point of Lotman's and Bakhtin's comments is that transmission models of communication cannot adequately account for many of the social and individual processes we wish to address. Instead, the dynamics of dialogism outlined by both will often come into play. In accordance with Lotman's notion of functional dualism, however, this does not mean that one should simply dismiss the transmission model as inadequate and replace it with one grounded in his ideas about the dialogicality of texts and in Bakhtin's ideas about internally persuasive discourse. Texts may simultaneously serve different functions.

In the final analysis, for any text the univocal and dialogic functions are best thought of as being in a kind of dynamic tension. There is always an element of univocality as envisioned in the transmission model and an element of response and retort as envisioned by Bakhtin. Put differently, for communication to occur, one must always listen to what the speaker says, but what the speaker says does not mechanistically generate an exclusive interpretation. This point about dynamic tension is tied to sociocultural contexts because such contexts serve to shape which of Lotman's two functions will predominate.

One of the criticisms most commonly leveled at Bakhtin is that he provided few detailed interpretations of texts and little concrete detail about the semiotic phenomena he had in mind. A phenomenon he did examine in some detail, however, and a phenomenon that is of use in trying to understand intermental and intramental functioning in sociocultural settings is "reported speech." Reported speech is the mechanism whereby one voice (the "reporting voice") reports the utterance of another (the "reported voice"). It was of particular interest to Bakhtin (Voloshinov, 1973) because it is an arena in which voices come into contact in one of several ways. Hence it is an arena in which one can explore issues such as the univocality or dialogicality of texts, authoritative and internally persuasive discourse, and other related issues. In what follows, I shall make no attempt to provide a comprehensive review of the issues of reported speech. Furthermore, I shall make no attempt to deal with the myriad issues being taken up by contemporary authors as a result of Bakhtin's claims about reported speech (Hickmann, 1985; Lucy, in press). Instead, I shall limit my comments to outlining some basic issues that will be of use when dealing with social and psychological processes in sociocultural context.

As a way of explicating reported speech, consider 1 as an utterance to be reported.

(1) I will be there!

In English, there are many possible ways to report this utterance. One of the basic forms involves "direct discourse" (Voloshinov, 1973) as in 2, and a second involves "indirect discourse" as in 3.

(2) He said, "I will be there!"
(3) He said enthusiastically that he would be here.

In 2 the reporting and reported voices are separated by the comma and quotation marks. Beyond the fact that utterances from the two voices are juxtaposed, there is little contact between them. As a result, the form of 1, including the intonation contour as marked by the exclamation point, is preserved in 2. In such cases the tendency in reporting speech is to "maintain the integrity and authenticity" of the reported utterance. In Bakhtin's view "[a] language may strive to forge hard and fast boundaries for reported speech. In such a case, the patterns and their modifications serve to demarcate the reported speech as clearly as possible, to screen it from penetration by the author's intonations, and to condense and enhance its individual linguistic characteristics" (Voloshinov, 1973, p. 119).

In contrast, in 3 there are several points of contact and interanimation between the reporting and reported voices. In this case there is a tendency for the reporting voice to "infiltrate" the reported utterance (Voloshinov, 1973, p. 120). Such infiltration and the "double voicedness" that ensues can occur in many guises. In 3, which is a relatively straightforward, unstylized case of indirect discourse, it appears in four places. The first is the second "he," an expression that is coreferential with "I" in the original utterance 1 but has a different form. Second, it appears in "would" in 3, a term that replaces "will" in 1. Third, the "here" in 3 replaces the "there" in 1 because the spatial coordinates of utterances 1 and 3 differ. Finally, the exclamation point in 1 is replaced with the adverb "enthusiastically" in 3.

Not all the changes in 1 to form 3 need to take the particular form they have in this example. But changes of the sort I have outlined invariably do, and indeed (because of the grammar of English), must take place when using indirect discourse to report an utterance.

For my purposes the major point does not concern details of syntax and pragmatics; instead, it is how one would answer the Bakhtinian question "Who is doing the talking?" in the case of utterance 3. Indirect discourse reveals a particular way in which the answer to this question is played out. For example, if one asks who is doing the talking in the case of the "he," "would," and "here" in 3, the answer must be that at least two voices are simultaneously involved. The voice that produced the reported utterance specifies the referent in each case, and the voice that produced the reporting utterance provides the particular way of identifying the referent, the "referential perspective" (Wertsch, 1980). One hears two voices in each case.

The use of "enthusiastically" in 3 reflects another way in which voices can come into contact in indirect discourse. One cannot simply duplicate the intonation contour or use an exclamation point in 3 in order to portray the affective tone of 1. The use of these devices fails because their significance attaches to the reporting rather than the reported voice. Instead, indirect discourse relies on an "analytic spirit" to represent this information. In Bakhtin's view, "analysis is the heart and soul of indirect discourse" (Voloshinov, 1973, p. 129). With regard to 3, this analytic orientation is manifested in the fact that the reporting voice infiltrates the reported voice by transforming the intonation contour or exclamation point of the reported voice into an analytic category. The reporting voice is allowed a wider range of options, and hence is given more responsibility in this case than in the case of the other three items, something that is revealed by the fact that expressions such as "said excitedly" or "shouted" could have been used in place of "said enthusiastically."

The relationship between authority and the various types of reported speech can be seen in many discourse settings. One that is of great contemporary interest concerns the way the news media report the utterances of others. Debate over this issue is often framed in terms of "accuracy," but unless the only form of reported speech is direct discourse (and even here), the notion of accuracy is not a simple one. The use of indirect discourse specifically calls on reporting voices to come into contact and interanimate reported voices in a variety of ways. In such instances, it is not the case that language functions "to forge hard and fast boundaries for reported speech" or "to screen it from penetration by the author's intonations, and to condense and enhance its individual linguistic characteristics. (Voloshinov, 1973, p. 119). Instead, the reporting voice interanimates the reported voice and invokes the "analytic spirit" mentioned by Voloshinov.

By employing the mechanisms characteristic of indirect discourse, therefore, the reporting voice becomes heavily involved in conveying what others have said. Once we become aware of this fact, the extent to which we rely on reporting voices in obtaining the news becomes quite striking. A casual examination of many western newspapers reveals that we, in fact, often have very little direct access to what was actually said by reported voices.

The tendency in the news media to rely heavily on indirect discourse reflects basic assumptions about the authority of reported and reporting voices, specifically, that the voices of those whose utterances are being reported do not have overwhelming authority in the context of today's media practices. In contrast to authoritative discourse, which "cannot be represented—it is only transmitted" (Bakhtin, 1981, p. 344), reporting voices (such as news reporters) typically feel quite free to summarize and delete portions of utterances, to invoke the "analytic spirit" reflected in terms such as "admitted" and "confided," and generally to rely more heavily on their own voices than on the voice being reported.

This tendency was not always present in western news media, and it certainly was not characteristic of the news media in Bakhtin's sociocultural context. As a striking counterexample to the interanimation of voices found in the media in contemporary America, we might consider the form in which utterances, such as speeches by Stalin and other official figures, were reported in the Soviet press before the age of *glasnost*. The standard procedure was to report a text verbatim in its entirety. Indeed, the text reported was typically supplied in written form to the media by the reported voice or representatives of that voice. In this way, virtually all indications of the reporting voice were deleted. Indeed, the identity of the news reporter was often not revealed in newspapers at all.

This practice resulted in long newspaper articles in which only very minimal evidence of a reporting voice emerged. In the case of many speeches reported in Soviet papers such as *Pravda*, the only evidence of a reporting voice is the comment, "Long and enthusiastic applause." That such comments by a reporting voice were set off with spaces, parentheses, and even italics served to emphasize the fact that the discourse was authoritative and that it allowed no interanimation by other voices. As such it allowed "no play with its borders, no gradual and flexible transitions, no spontaneously creative stylizing variants on it" (Bakhtin, 1981, p. 343).

I would stress that there is much more to Bakhtin's account of reported speech and its relation to authoritative and internally persuasive discourse than what I have outlined here. He went well beyond the basic distinction between indirect and direct discourse, delving into the structures and functions of "quasi-direct" and "quasi-indirect" speech, and he traced the history of the uses of these various devices in national languages and in the social language of novelistic discourse.

My major point is that reported speech provides a concrete example of how voices may or may not come into contact, interanimate, and infiltrate one another in various ways. Furthermore, this interanimation can be expected to occur to a greater or lesser degree depending on whether the reported utterance occurs in the form of authoritative or internally persuasive discourse. Whereas authoritative discourse tends to discourage contact, internally persuasive discourse encourages it.

The Role of Literal Meaning in a Bakhtinian Approach to Meaning

The notion of "literal meaning" is at the core of most contemporary linguistic analyses of meaning. It is a notion that is so obvious to most writers and readers that it is seldom defined explicitly, even in encyclopedic works on semantics such as Lyons (1977). Instead, it is simply contrasted with other notions such as "figurative meaning" or "metaphorical meaning."

Since the dawn of linguistic studies, however, there has been a group of scholars, often quite small, that has questioned the "obvious" notion of literal meaning. In recent years, this group has included Goffman (1976), Linell (1982), Rommetveit (1988), and Taylor (1985a). Recognizing that "issues concerning literalness of meaning range all the way from folk linguistics to axiomatic features of formalized semantic theory" (Rommetveit, 1988, p. 13), these scholars have called for special, explicit treatment of this notion. They recognize that the idea of literal meaning is grounded in what have become everyday practices in the western world having to do with literacy and modern scientific rationality. These have come to form such a pervasive part of modern life (especially among those who *write* about literal meaning), it is now very difficult to recognize that "the assumption that there is such a thing as the strict and literal meaning of an expression turns out to be an ethnocentric assumption" (Taylor, 1985a, p. 289).

Like Linell (1982) and Rommetveit (1988), Bakhtin traced our willingness to accept literal meaning as some kind of underlying standard to the authority of those who have studied it over the centuries. He argued, for example, that the widespread appeal of the "abstract objectivism" of figures such as Descartes and Saussure can be traced at least in part to the fact that "the first philologists and the first linguists were always and everywhere priests" and that "European linguistic thought formed and matured over concern with the cadavers of written language" (Voloshinov, 1973, pp. 41, 71, 74).

Regardless of the source of its widespread acceptance, from a Bakhtinian perspective the notion of literal meaning is problematic for several reasons. Primary among them, it is tied to linguistic segments taken out of context. As Goffman (1976) has noted, literal meaning is grounded in pretheoretical assumptions such as "the common-sense notion . . . that the word *in isolation* will have a general basic, or most down-to-earth meaning" (p. 303). Such assumptions clearly run counter to those that underlay Bakhtin's translinguistic analyses, which focus on the utterance as "the *real unit* of speech communication" (Bakhtin, 1986, p. 71). In particular, such ideas about literal meaning make it next to impossible to consider the issue of addressivity, which played such a central role in Bakhtin's analysis; they encourage investigators to treat expressions as if they "belong to nobody and are addressed to nobody" (p. 99).

In a Bakhtinian approach to meaning, however, "any utterance is a link in the chain of speech communication" (p. 84) and "utterances are not indifferent to one another, and are not self-sufficient; they are aware of and mutually reflect one another" (p. 91). Bakhtin's approach thus rules out the acceptance of literal meaning as a presupposed given. A level of analysis concerned with voice and dialogicality cannot somehow be added on to an account of literal meaning; rather, the categories of voice and dialogicality are fundamental building blocks.

Where does a Bakhtinian approach leave the notion of literal meaning? Although it may at first appear that it simply makes literal meaning a useless category, I do not think this is its message. Literal meaning can certainly exist within this framework but not in some kind of *a priori* way. Instead, it is seen as a kind of meaning generated by a particular semiotic activity and a particular social language, namely the social language that concerns itself with the kinds of reflective activity found in modern, rational, literate discourse. The notion of literal meaning is thus part of a modern "linguistic ideology" (Silverstein, 1987) that privileges a particular view of language and language activity.

Bakhtin's refusal to ground his account of meaning in literalness in no way reflects a lack of awareness of systematicity in meaning. He certainly did not believe that any utterance can have any meaning. Instead, his search for systematicity was grounded in the regularities of social languages. He made this point explicitly in connection with speech genres.

> When we select words in the process of constructing an utterance, we by no means always take them from the system of language in their neutral *dictionary* form. We usually take them from *other utterances,* and mainly from utterances that are kindred to ours in genre, that is, in theme, composition, or style. Consequently, we choose words according to their generic specifications. A speech genre is not a form of language, but a typical form of utterance; as such the genre also includes a certain typical kind of expression that inheres in it. In the genre the word acquires a particular typical expression. Genres correspond to typical situations of speech communication, typical themes, and, consequently, also to particular contacts between the *meanings* of words and actual concrete reality under certain typical circumstances. (1986, p. 87)

Thus types, or categories, of *utterances,* rather than equivalence relationships derived by abstracting linguistic expressions from their contexts of use form the basis of Bakhtin's approach to meaning. It is by appropriating, or populating, social languages and speech genres that utterances take on their meaning.

An Illustration

As a way of summarizing and coordinating my comments on the disengaged image of the self, the functional dualism of texts, authority and text, and literal meaning, I shall turn to an example concerned with the socialization of mental functioning. This example illustrates what Bakhtin labeled the "primordial dialogism of discourse" (1981, p. 275). By this he meant the dialogic processes involved in concrete, face-to-face communication. In particular, the illustration concerns the ways in which the dialogic organization of speech on the intermental plane is mastered, thereby shaping the intramental plane of functioning.

The intramental functioning that results from this mastery, or "internalization" (Wertsch and Stone, 1985), is closely related to what Bakhtin termed "hidden dialogicality," which he characterized as follows: "Imagine a dialogue of two persons in which the statements of the second speaker are omitted, but in such a way that the general sense is not at all violated. The second speaker is present invisibly, his words are not there, but deep traces left by these words have a determining influence on all the present and visible words of the first speaker. We sense that this is a conversation, although only one person is speaking, and it is a conversation of the most intense kind, for each present, uttered word responds and reacts with its every fiber to the invisible speaker, points to something outside itself, beyond its own limits, to the unspoken words of another person" (1984, p. 197).

The case of hidden dialogicality I shall examine involves the interaction of a two-and-a-half-year-old, middle-class American child and her mother in a problem-solving setting. The following excerpts reflect the microgenetic transitions that occurred over the course of one interactional session, whose object was to insert pieces from a "pieces pile" into a "copy" puzzle so that it would be identical with a "model" puzzle. The data for this illustration come from three "episodes" of interaction, which I shall define as verbal and nonverbal interaction in connection with the identification, selection, and insertion of a piece in the copy puzzle. In all three episodes the correct location of the piece in the copy puzzle could be determined only by consulting the model puzzle. I shall give special attention to the initial phase of each episode, which included the strategic substep of consulting the model puzzle in order to determine where the piece should go in the copy puzzle.

The initial segment of the first episode between this mother (M) and the child (C) proceeded as follows:

(1) C: Oh. (*C glances at the model puzzle, C looks at the pieces pile.*) Oh, now where's this one go? (*C picks up a black piece from the pieces pile, C looks at the copy puzzle, C looks at the pieces pile.*)

(2) M: Where does it go on this other one? (*C puts the black piece she is holding back down in the pieces pile. C looks at the pieces pile.*)

(3) M: Look at the other truck and then you can tell. (*C looks at the model puzzle, C glances at the pieces pile, C looks at the model puzzle, C glances at the pieces pile.*)

(4) C: Well . . . (*C looks at the copy puzzle, C looks at the model puzzle.*)

(5) C: I look at it.

(6) C: Um, this other puzzle has a black one over there. (*C points to the black piece in the model puzzle.*)

While it is true that the child glanced at the model puzzle at the very beginning of this episode, it does not appear that she did so at that point to determine where a piece should go in the copy puzzle. The first time she consulted the model for some clear purpose was in response to the mother's utterances 2 and 3. This response is part of a dialogue that occurred on the intermental plane of functioning. The child's responses 4, 5, and 6 indicate that in one sense she could respond appropriately to the mother's directive, while in another sense she apparently had not understood or incorporated the reasoning that motivated her mother's question because she did not see where her mother was going with the line of questioning.

The initial segment of a subsequent episode between this mother and child proceeded as follows:

(7) C: (*C glances at the pieces pile, C looks at the copy puzzle, C picks up the orange piece from the pieces pile.*) Now where do you think the orange one goes?

(8) M: Where does it go on the other truck? (*C looks at the model puzzle.*)

(9) C: Right there. (*C points to the orange piece in the model puzzle.*) The orange one goes right there.

In this episode the child's action, consulting the model puzzle, was again part of the dialogue on the intermental plane. But the fact that the mother did not have to follow up her first directive with a second one, such as utterance 3 in the first episode, indicates that the child had begun to understand where the mother was going with her line of questioning.

A third episode in this problem-solving process began as follows:

(10) C: (*C looks at the pieces pile, C picks up the yellow piece from the pieces pile, C looks at the copy puzzle.*) Now how . . . Now where . . . Now . . . (*C looks at the model puzzle.*)

(11) C: You . . . you . . . the yellow on that side goes . . . One yellow one's right next there. (*C points to the yellow piece in the model puzzle, C looks at the yellow piece she is holding in her hand.*)

(12) M: Okay.

In this episode the mother did not ask a question to guide the child's gaze to the model puzzle (intermental plane). Instead, it now appears that the child's egocentric and inner speech (intramental plane) guided this process. In Bakhtin's terminology, the child's speech has taken on the properties of hidden dialogicality. The "statements of the second speaker [the mother] are omitted," but the "second speaker is present invisibly"; her "words are not there, but deep traces left by these words have a determining influence on all the present and visible words of the first speaker [the child]." Furthermore, as predicted by Vygotsky (1987), the egocentric speech utterances have taken on an abbreviated, predicative form (Wertsch, 1979b). Instead of being fully developed answers, the child's responses to the "unspoken words of another person" appear in the form of abbreviated utterances, a fact that reflects the beginning of the differentiation of speech for oneself and speech for others.

A comparison of these three episodes reveals several important microgenetic transitions in the child's mediated action. The first two began with the child's question about where a piece should go (utterances 1 and 7) and the mother's response, which directed the child's attention to the model puzzle (utterances 2, 3, and 8). In both of these episodes, the child's original questions led to the mother's response, which, in turn, led to the child's response, consulting the model. All of these communicative moves were carried out through external social dialogue (dialogue on the intermental plane). But the third episode began quite differently. First, the child did not produce a fully ex-panded question about where a piece should go (although it appears that she began to do so in utterance 10). Second, and more important, when she looked at the model puzzle after utterance 10, it was not in response to an adult's directive in overt social dialogue. She did not rely on the adult to provide a regulative utterance but presupposed the utterance that would have occurred on the intermental plane and responded in egocentric and inner dialogue.

There are striking similarities between several of the child's utter-ances: 6 in the first episode, 9 in the second, and 11 in the third.

First episode
> (6) C: Um, this other puzzle has a black one over there. (*C points to the black piece in the model puzzle.*)

Second episode
> (9) C: Right there. (*C points to the orange piece in the model puzzle.*)
> The orange one goes right there.

Third episode
> (11) C: You . . . you . . . the yellow on that side goes . . . One yellow one's right next there. (*C points to the yellow piece in the model puzzle, C looks at the yellow piece she is holding in her hand.*)

In all three cases, the verbal and nonverbal behaviors comprise a state-ment about the location of a particular piece in the model puzzle. In addition, in terms of the sequences of behaviors in the three episodes, 6, 9, and 11 mediate similar aspects of the problem-solving action. In all three cases the utterance serves to advance this action in the same way (all are concerned with consulting the model to determine where a piece from the pieces pile should go).

The striking similarity between utterance 11 and the previous two, despite the fact that 11 is part of intramental functioning and the others of intermental functioning, is due to the fact that all three utterances are responses to questions. In the case of 11, however, the question is posed by the child rather than the mother. An abbreviated form of this question appears in utterance 10. In subsequent episodes, the only utterances that appear in overt speech are the "answers"; no questions surface, even in abbreviated form.

This tendency to see "answers" in children's speech in the absence of questions is not uncommon in such problem-solving settings (Wertsch, 1979a). The fact that the utterances seem so obviously to be answers raises several issues that can be adequately addressed only if we invoke some notion of dialogicality. The main reason these utterances seem to be answers is that they mediate the action in ways that are similar to utterances in earlier episodes that *were* replies to concrete, overt questions. That is, the genetic precursor to these "answers" on the intramental plane can be found in intermental functioning.

If this is so, how does one understand the notion of a question in such cases? Vygotsky's writings suggest that the questions to which the "answers" correspond now occur in inner speech. This does not mean that a full-blown version of each question is somehow represented (perhaps subvocally) in internal mental functioning. Indeed, Vygotsky went to great pains in his account of the abbreviation that characterizes inner speech to preclude such a conclusion. Instead, the question is *presupposed*. The meaning of the answer, as it occurs in the flow of problem-solving activity, changes to reflect the question that had formerly been part of an overt, social interaction.

This point has also been made by other Soviet investigators in their account of inner speech. In particular, P. Ya. Gal'perin (1969) has argued for the notion of presupposition in his account of the formation of mental acts. In his view, inner speech is inherently grounded in the notion of presupposition, which allows one to address the issue of how an utterance reflects the context of the other utterances among which it is situated.

Bakhtin's account of dialogicality can provide essential insights into several aspects of this interaction. His approach suggests that what comes to be incorporated into, or presupposed by, an utterance are voices that were formerly represented explicitly in intermental functioning. The issue is how one voice comes into contact with another, thereby changing the meaning of what it is saying by becoming increasingly dialogical, or multivoiced.

This conclusion is diametrically opposed to the notion that the process of microgenetic change can be understood simply as the shift from dialogue to monologue. While this may be a way of characterizing external, observable behaviors in the transition from intermental to intramental functioning, it fails to recognize the increasing dialogicality that characterizes intramental processes. Processes such as this (that is, "dialogization") led Vygotsky (1981b) to assert that even on the intramental plane, mental functioning retains a "quasi-social" nature.

The process of dialogization poses a special set of problems for a theory of meaning. It calls on such a theory, for example, to account for the fact that in the mother-child interaction discussed above, utterances 6, 9, and 11 are overtly quite similar and mediate action in a similar way but are fundamentally different in the degree of dialogization they involve. This is a problem that most existing theories of meaning have no way of addressing, but it is a central one for a sociocultural approach to mind.

The implications of the process of dialogization can be summarized in terms of the four issues outlined in this chapter. First, it is impossible to understand the transitions involved if one begins with an approach to meaning that rests on a disengaged image of the self and the atomism associated with it. These transitions involve changes in speech over the course of the interaction, changes which reflect the impact of what Taylor (1985a) terms "outside interference" or "subordination to outside authority." As I outlined earlier, this outside authority can be understood in terms of Bakhtin's claim that the "word is half someone else's." If we ask the Bakhtinian question "Who is doing the talking?," the hidden dialogicality found in the later episodes of the mother-child interaction I have described leads one to say that *both* the adult and child are speaking. In an important sense, then, the meaning of the child's utterances reflects the outside interference of another's voice.

Second, the illustration provides several examples of how the functional dualism of texts outlined by Lotman operates in the genetic transitions involved. A transmission model of communication cannot alone account for these transitions. While it is certainly true that information is conveyed from adult to child and vice versa, it is obvious that the adult's utterances also served as a "thinking device," a mechanism "to generate new meanings" for the child. The text of the two participants' utterances is "a semiotic space in which languages interact, interfere, and organize themselves hierarchically" (Lotman, 1988b, p. 37). This is not to say that the influence occurs only in one direction, from the adult to the child; the adult's utterances can themselves only be understood as responses to the child's. But according to the hierarchical organization mentioned by Lotman, the main locus of change was in the child's speech and thinking.

This touches on a third issue, authority and text. Although the meanings of the child's utterances (and hence her understanding) underwent a major microgenetic transition over the course of the interaction, the meaning of the adult's utterances did not. The child's utterances changed in that they increasingly reflected the hidden dialogicality derived from incorporating the mother's meanings into her own. In contrast, the mother's voice remained relatively impermeable; she did not change her meanings or understanding of the strategic task as a result of her dialogue with the child. As in the case of the terms "outside interference" and "subordination to outside authority," the use of the term "authoritative" here need not imply some kind of overt or potentially punitive force. Instead, these terms are concerned with the ways in which the dynamics between voices are played out as these voices come into contact.

Finally, it is quite apparent that an approach to meaning that is based on the notion of literal meaning cannot account for the microgenetic transitions involved in the adult-child interaction reviewed here. For example, although the similarity of utterances 6, 9, and 11 noted above can be captured by an account of literal meaning, the essence of the microgenetic change involved is that, in an important sense, these three utterances do *not* have the same meaning. It is only by noting the quite different relations they have to the mother's utterances (that is, the increasing level of hidden dialogicality) that we can describe the changes in intermental and intramental functioning.

This example of microgenetic transition and the ways it is related to these four issues of meaning serves as a first step in outlining the kinds of phenomena that can be examined from the perspective of a Bakhtinian approach to meaning. It allows the examination of the same concrete issues of dialogicality, but it is also limited in several essential respects. Most important, it has little to say about ways in which mental functioning shapes and is shaped by institutional, historical, and cultural contexts. This issue provides the focus of the remaining chapters.

5

The Heterogeneity of Voices

In this chapter I shall return to the analogy Vygotsky made between tools and semiotic mediation and expand on it in light of several of the ideas discussed in Chapters 3 and 4. As Vygotsky noted, the analogy between technical tools and psychological tools has its limitations. In my view, however, he did not push this analogy far enough. In particular, he did not use it to examine the *diversity* of mediational means available to human beings. In this connection I would suggest that mediational means be viewed not as some kind of single, undifferentiated whole but rather, in terms of the diverse items that make up a *tool kit*.

Vygotsky did not address this issue in these terms, but at several points in his writings he suggested something along these lines. He noted, for example, that "the following can serve as examples of psychological tools and their complex systems: language; various systems for counting; mnemonic techniques; algebraic symbol systems; works of art; writing; schemes, diagrams, maps, and mechanical drawings; all sorts of conventional signs; and so on" (1981a, p. 137). Furthermore, within the most important form of mediational means in his account—human natural language—he recognized the possibility of decontextualization as manifested in scientific concepts and the possibility of linguistic conceptualization as manifested in inner speech, the two basic semiotic potentials outlined in Chapter 2. Despite the attention he devoted to the diversity of mediational means, however, he did not deal with many of the implications of explicitly viewing psychological tools as part of the larger organized whole of a tool kit.

If we incorporate the notion of a tool kit into Vygotsky's approach, action continues to be shaped by mediational means but several new questions arise: what is the nature of the diversity of mediational means and why is one, as opposed to another, mediational means employed in carrying out a particular form of action? Such questions will help to determine the shape a sociocultural approach to mediated action will take, in particular, how cultural, historical, and institutional differences in mental action are to be understood.

These differences have often been formulated in terms of whether members of a group "have" or do not "have" certain forms of mental capacity. It has often been asserted, for example, that various groups do not have higher order thinking, or a concept of freedom or guilt. Although assessments like these are often encountered in folk theories and stereotypic judgments, they are not uncommon in the discourse of scientific psychology and other social science disciplines as well.

The set of assumptions underlying the metaphor of possession has been called into question by a variety of recent studies in developmental psychology (Donaldson, 1978; Rogoff, 1990), cross-cultural psychology (Cole and Scribner, 1974), "everyday cognition" (Lave, 1988; Rogoff and Lave, 1984), and other areas of social science inquiry. In general, these studies have shown that children and adults who were not thought to have a particular ability on the basis of an assessment in one context did in fact demonstrate that ability in other contexts. This is not to say that anyone can demonstrate any ability given the right contextual conditions. What it does say, however, is that the metaphor of possession—a metaphor grounded solidly in the atomistic assumption that in the end individuals either have or do not have an ability—is now recognized as severely limited.

A tool kit approach allows group and contextual differences in mediated action to be understood in terms of the array of mediational means to which people have access and the patterns of choice they manifest in selecting a particular means for a particular occasion. This is a natural extension of claims in earlier chapters about the nature of mediated action and mediated agency.

A tool kit approach to mediated action is consistent with the observation that differences in mental functioning between one group and another are often not so much a matter of distinct processes as they are a matter of the same process (for example, mode of reasoning) used in different contexts. This point is especially important in considering the endless, often bogus arguments about whether or not a group "has" a particular concept or schema, or some other form of mental functioning. In a typical debate, dissenters "refute" the claim that a group does not have a capacity by showing that, in at least one context, the members of the group in question can indeed demonstrate mastery of the mental function at issue.

As long as the metaphor of possession shapes the debate, a basic issue—the different uses or functions of a tool—escapes the attention of those involved, and they often find themselves in the somewhat ridiculous position of claiming that there are no differences between groups that are obviously different. If the argument is formulated in terms of a tool kit analogy, however, with the understanding that different groups may employ similar tools in different ways, much of this confusion can be avoided.

One of the clearest illustrations of how a tool kit approach can clarify matters can be found in the literature of developmental psychology, where "different groups" typically means children at different levels of maturity. As often happens, after one investigator has asserted that only children above a certain developmental level can carry out some task, other investigators document the successful performance of the same task by younger children in a context different from the one originally examined, thereby "refuting" the original claim. Margaret Donaldson's (1978) studies of children's performance on Piagetian tasks are a case in point. In study after study she demonstrated that when a task makes "human sense," children at an earlier developmental stage than that predicted by Piaget can carry it out successfully. Analogous examples can be found in the studies of Cole and Scribner (1974), two investigators who have done a great deal to dispel misleading claims about parallels between the mental functioning of adults in traditional cultures and children in modern western cultures.

For all too many investigators, the results of studies like these have been understood, in narrowly methodological terms, as deriving from clever techniques that reveal what subjects "really" know (that is, "have"). To interpret these findings in this way, however, is to invoke the possession metaphor in a way not intended by Donaldson or Cole and Scribner; it assumes that by using the right methods these researchers have simply been able to show that children or adults from traditional cultures really *do* have a mental process and hence are similar to older children or adults in modern societies. In the eyes of these researchers, to demonstrate that one group of subjects can perform a task in one context that another group can perform in a different context is by no means intended simply to refute the notion that there are differences between groups; important differences between such groups obviously remain. As I shall suggest, they can be understood in terms of how subjects recognize and create contexts by using various items from a tool kit.

The tool kit analogy represents an extension of my basic claims about the need to place mediated action and mediated agency at the center of our analyses. What is new is that, in addition to recognizing that the agent is the individual(s)-operating-with-mediational-means, there is a need to provide some account of why one of several possible mediational means is employed on a particular occasion. Given that the selection and use of mediational means is assumed not to be random, some sort of an account of the organization of mediational means is required.

I would emphasize that this line of reasoning does not assume that differences in the level of mastery of mediational means are unimportant and that the selection of a mediational means is the only dynamic at issue. In my view, however, the possession metaphor has come to dominate the discourse on these issues to such a degree that it often blinds us to other accounts of how and why people are different in their mental functioning.

In order to address these issues, I want to extend Vygotsky's account of mediation by exploring the tool kit analogy. My account will revolve around two basic problems: first, the notion of "heterogeneity," a notion developed, or redeveloped, by Peeter Tulviste (1978, 1986, 1987, 1988), which contributes to a general framework for understanding the nature of a tool kit; and second, the implications of a sociocultural approach to meaning (see Chapter 4) for a tool kit approach.

Heterogeneity

In his account of verbal thinking, Tulviste (1986) has addressed what I am here terming a tool kit approach under the heading *heterogeneity:* "The phenomenon of the heterogeneity of verbal thinking (or 'cognitive pluralism') consists of the fact that in any culture and in any individual there exists not one, homogeneous form of thinking, but different types of verbal thinking" (p. 19). Tulviste has borrowed the term "heterogeneity" from Lévy-Bruhl (1923), noting an essential assumption in the latter's use of this term: *qualitatively different* forms of thinking exist. By assuming this rather than that different forms could be distinguished strictly according to some quantitative dimension (for example, stages in a single developmental hierarchy), Lévy-Bruhl was able to generate several insights, which, as Tulviste points out, have often been overlooked or misinterpreted. In particular, it led Lévy-Bruhl to argue that "the intellectual activity of primitive man is not a lower, less-developed form of 'our' intellectual activity (as Spencer and other evolutionists asserted), but is qualitatively different from the latter" (Tulviste, 1987, p. 7).

As Tulviste notes, scholars have long employed some version of a notion of heterogeneity of thinking, but, on balance, heterogeneity has been given relatively little attention in most schools of psychology, even though an understanding of it might suggest solutions to many of the intractable issues these schools have addressed. Tulviste finds it particularly surprising that it has not been a topic of investigation in analyses of historical and cross-cultural differences.

Of the positions that have been taken on heterogeneity, some focus on thinking, others focus on something more specific, such as verbal thinking, and still others cast their discussion in terms of behavior. These differences are significant, especially because certain forms of heterogeneity can be distinguished from others on the basis of what is being ranked. What unites the work of the philosophers and psychologists I shall review is the opinion that a fundamental characteristic of human activity is the existence of a variety of qualitatively different forms of representing and acting on the world.

The three major positions on heterogeneity I shall outline differ in their view of how thinking, verbal thinking, behavior, or whatever, are organized, both in terms of genesis and in terms of power or efficacy. The first position views forms of representation and action as ranked, both genetically and in terms of power or efficacy; indeed, these two kinds of ranking are collapsed so that whatever emerges later is assumed to be inherently more powerful. This position, which I shall term *heterogeneity as genetic hierarchy,* can be summarized by saying that "later" is viewed as more powerful (and often, at least implicitly, as better). The second position assumes that forms of representation and action can be ranked genetically, but this does not mean that later forms are assumed to be more powerful. This position, which I shall term *heterogeneity despite genetic hierarchy,* can be summarized by saying that although some forms of functioning emerge later than others, they are not inherently better. Finally, the third position claims that there is no inherent ranking, either in terms of genesis or in terms of power, of the various forms of representation and action in human mental functioning. This is a position that I shall term *nongenetic heterogeneity*.

Heterogeneity as Genetic Hierarchy

As Tulviste (1986) observes, when the heterogeneity of verbal thinking has been addressed at all in psychology, it has usually been seen as a problem involving different stages in a developmental hierarchy. According to this view, "having attained higher stages in the development of thinking, humans sometimes nonetheless drop to lower levels, to already completed stages of ontogenesis or sociogenesis [i.e., sociocultural history] . . . It is held that the completed stages in the development of thinking are not lost without a trace, but are preserved, and the return to them is viewed as regression" (p. 19). Here, developmentally later phases are seen as inherently higher in terms of power or efficacy. I would note the terms "drop" and "regression" in Tulviste's summary of this position, which often uses terms such as "higher," "levels," and "primitive" in a relatively undifferentiated way, one that does not distinguish between being developmentally higher and being higher in terms of power or efficacy.

A commitment to the notion of heterogeneity as genetic hierarchy is evident in the writings of several major developmental psychologists. One of the basic assumptions behind Werner's approach was that "man possesses more than one level of behavior" (1948, p. 39); that is, human mental functioning is characterized by heterogeneity and this heterogeneity is organized in terms of a genetic hierarchy. As he states, "the normal adult, even at our own cultural level, does not always act on the higher levels of behavior. His mental structure is marked by not one but many functional patterns, one lying above the other. Because of this the isolated individual, genetically considered, must occasionally exhibit in his varying behavior different phases of development" (p. 38). This assumption surfaces at many points in Werner's writings. It was explicit in his genetic experiments on "primitivation," and it provided the framework within which he approached issues such as the pathologically primitive (for example, schizophrenic) structure of human personality. With regard to the role of genetic ranking in the everyday activity of normal western adults, Allport's comments in his foreword to Werner's *Comparative Psychology of Mental Development* are instructive: "No matter how confidently we pride ourselves on our logical acumen and capacity for scientific inference, our thought too turns out to be primitive much of the time. While tactfully confining himself to children, primitives, and psychotics, the author tells us in a sly way more than a little about our own mental lives" (1948, p. xii).

Vygotsky addressed the issue of heterogeneity most specifically in his analysis of concept development, yet his comments on this issue reveal a certain ambivalence in his thinking. In some cases, he seemed to assume that heterogeneity does not exist, since there is a powerful tendency for later forms of mental functioning to transform and incorporate earlier forms: "thanks to the mastery of this new structure [i.e., of scientific concepts], [a child] rebuilds and transforms the structure of all previous concepts . . . The formal discipline of studying in scientific concepts results in the transformation of the child's entire sphere of spontaneous concepts. The major significance of scientific concepts in the history of children's mental development consists of this" (1982b, pp. 280–287).

Elsewhere in his writings, however, Vygotsky seems to have assumed that earlier forms of speaking and thinking are not always transformed and incorporated by later forms. In this connection he argued that even with the emergence of genuine and scientific concepts, humans continue to have access to everyday concepts and, indeed, often employ the latter: "children who have mastered a higher form of thinking— [genuine] concepts, by no means leave more elementary forms behind. For a long time these elementary forms remain the quantitatively predominant and leading type of thinking in many areas of children's experience. Even in the case of adults, as we have noted earlier, it is far from always the case that they think in concepts. Their thinking often is carried out on the level of complexes, sometimes dropping to still more elementary, more primitive forms" (p. 176).

This formulation clearly reflects Vygotsky's acceptance of a notion of heterogeneity as genetic hierarchy and seems to be more representative of his overall approach. It is something he specified in more detail in his use of an analogy from geology: "one cannot think of . . . the process of shifting among various forms of thinking and distinct phases in its development as a purely mechanistic process in which each new phase emerges when the previous one is completely finished and completed. The picture of development turns out to be much more complex. *Different genetic forms coexist,* just as in the earth's core the deposits of quite different geological epochs coexist" (1956, p. 204). This geological metaphor is one that Luria (1973) also employed in explicating various genetically organized levels of mental functioning. In particular, he used it in his analyses of the breakdown and remediation of neuropsychological functioning after brain injury.

There are strong parallels in Werner's, Vygotsky's, and Luria's treatment of heterogeneity. For all of them, however, heterogeneity exists because different genetic levels of functioning exist. In terms of the tool kit analogy, it is as if the tools are acquired in a certain order and are therefore *inherently* organized along a continuum from lower to higher, or from less powerful to more powerful. These theorists are also alike in that they say very little about when and why a subject would use anything less than the highest (that is, most powerful) form of mental functioning available.

The latter issue raises some very important questions that have puzzling, if not embarrassing, implications for all three approaches. In general, it would appear to be nonsensical to select a less powerful, and hence less appropriate, mediational means than is available to approach a task. As Tulviste notes, "it is incomprehensible why [lower forms of thinking] must be preserved when the 'savage' or child has mastered higher stages in the development of thinking" (1986, p. 19). This paradox remains the major unresolved issue for approaches that treat heterogeneity in terms of genetic hierarchy.

Heterogeneity despite Genetic Hierarchy

A second major position on heterogeneity holds that different forms of mental functioning or behavior emerge at different periods, but that later ones are not inherently more powerful or efficacious than earlier ones. As Tulviste points out, several theorists have taken this position. One of those he cites is William James.

In his chapter in *Pragmatism* called "Pragmatism and Common Sense," James deals with three types of thinking: common sense, science, and critical philosophy. Although he spoke of these as "levels" or "stages" that have emerged at different points in history, he refused to accept the assumption that one is inherently more powerful (or more *true*) than another.

> It is impossible . . . to say that any stage as yet in sight is absolutely more *true* than any other. Common sense is the more *consolidated* stage, because it got its innings first, and made all language into its ally . . . [However,] if common sense were true, why should science have had to brand the secondary qualities, to which our world owes all its living interest, as false, and to invent an invisible world of points and curves and mathematical equations instead? . . . But now

if the new kinds of scientific "thing," the corpuscular and etheric world, were essentially more "true," why should they have excited so much criticism within the body of science itself? (1916, pp. 190–191)

James's approach to the three types of thinking was based on a "pragmatistic view that all our theories are *instrumental*." These modes of mental functioning must be viewed as tools, or instruments, for dealing with particular tasks rather than as "revelations or gnostic answers to some divinely instituted world enigma" (p. 194). The upshot is that different forms of thinking are more appropriate for different spheres of human activity. "Common sense is *better* for one sphere of life, science for another, philosophic criticism for a third." On the issue of whether any one of these forms of thinking is inherently better in the sense of being truer, James answered, "Heaven only knows" (p. 190).

A particularly important aspect of James's approach is that he did not assume that common sense is somehow more primitive or lower than other forms of thinking. It is clearly genetically prior in his view (it "got its innings first"), yet this by no means implies that he viewed it as less efficacious or powerful. On the contrary, it "is *better* for one sphere of life." By separating genetic hierarchy from the hierarchy of power or efficacy, James's view is one of heterogeneity despite genetic hierarchy.

Building on other theoretical foundations, Tulviste (1986) has also developed a position of heterogeneity despite genetic hierarchy. His approach arises from his criticism of the psychology of thinking, child psychology, and educational psychology. Studies in these fields, he claims, tend to assume that "[more] developed forms of thinking can simply be equated with scientific [*nauchnyi*] thinking" (p. 24). This leads to the assumption that "pre-scientific" forms of thinking have no independent significance.

In contrast, Tulviste proposes an "activity-oriented" approach that shares certain underlying assumptions with the type of instrumentalism found in the pragmatistic approach outlined by James. According to this view,

there is an obvious connection between various forms of activity and the heterogeneity of thinking. This is true both between and within cultures. The reason for the heterogeneity of verbal thinking must not be sought in the accidental preservation in society or in the individual of "old," "lower," or "previous" sociogenetic [social historical] or ontogenetic stages of thinking. Instead, it must be sought in the multiplicity of activities that are distributed in society and carried out by the individual. Heterogeneity developed through social history such that with the development of material and mental production new forms of activity appeared. These new forms of activity required new types of thinking and gave rise to them. At the same time, to the degree that earlier forms of activity, which fulfill some role in the culture, are preserved, the "old" types of thinking that correspond to them are preserved and continue to function. (pp. 24–25)

Although Tulviste does not specifically address the issue of a pragmatic theory of truth, his notion of activity overlaps with the notion of a "sphere of life" that James mentioned in describing where common sense, science, and critical philosophy may be adequate and appropriate.

Tulviste makes a further claim about an unfounded assumption he sees in the work of many scholars who have tried to make cross-cultural or cross-historical comparisons. This is the assumption that it is possible to characterize an individual or a society on the basis of a particular type of activity and a corresponding form of thinking. As he states, "the tendency to make a global opposition between the thinking of people in one culture with that of people in another is misguided. Types of thinking correspond not with different cultures, but with different forms of activity. It is not reasonable to speak of primitive and civilized thinking; instead, it is reasonable to speak of common sensical (everyday, practical thinking), scientific thinking, artistic thinking, and so forth. The basis for such a division is the functional correspondence between certain types of thinking on the one hand and certain types of activity and the tasks that emerge and must be solved in the course of carrying out these activities" on the other (p. 27).

In terms of the tool kit approach to mediational means, the notion of heterogeneity despite genetic hierarchy translates into the view that different tools are acquired at different developmental stages, but they have no inherent ranking with regard to power or efficacy. Some tools are more powerful and efficacious for certain activities or spheres of life, and others are more powerful and efficacious for others.

Nongenetic Heterogeneity

Nongenetic heterogeneity, the third type, has in common with heterogeneity despite genetic hierarchy the assumption that there is no inherent ranking of the power or efficacy of psychological tools; different mediational means are viewed as being appropriate for different settings or tasks. But it differs in that, in this case, the variation in mediational means is not tied to development. Those approaches that can be grouped under the heading nongenetic heterogeneity may assume that development occurs *within* various psychological tools, but they do not view the forms themselves as being distinguished or ranked on the basis of order of appearance.

The work of Carol Gilligan (1982) provides a good example of an approach grounded in assumptions of nongenetic heterogeneity. Gilligan has argued that, as a result of much of the theorizing done in psychology, "the thinking of women is often classified with that of children" (p. 70). In contrast to such theorizing, which makes the implicit assumption that mental functioning can be ranked along a single continuum, she has called upon investigators to be more sensitive to the existence of qualitatively distinct forms of mental functioning, each of which has its own developmental path. In this connection, Gilligan writes of the "distinct moral language" she found in interviews with women about the dilemmas posed by abortion and states that its "evolution traces a sequence of development." This distinct moral language is grounded in an ethic of care, which defines moral problems in terms of the "obligation to exercise care and avoid hurt" (p. 73), in sharp contrast to a moral language concerned with abstract rights and the "logic of justice" (p. 30).

Gilligan argues that mature forms of thinking involve an interanimation of these two languages, but she assumes that each follows a somewhat independent genetic path during earlier phases of development. This recognition of a diversity that is not tied to genetic hierarchy puts Gilligan's approach in the category of nongenetic heterogeneity. A tool kit based on a view such as Gilligan's, therefore, would include several items that can be ranked neither in terms of genesis nor in terms of power or efficacy. The various tools (in this case, "languages") are presumed to emerge and develop largely independently of one another.

The Tool Kit Analogy and Bakhtin

When the notion of heterogeneity is considered from the perspective of a Bakhtinian approach to meaning (see Chapter 4), it raises a host of challenges and claims, foremost among them the question of how to distinguish one tool from another. When one considers Vygotsky's list of psychological tools ("language; various systems for counting; mnemonic techniques; algebraic symbol systems; works of art; writing; schemes, diagrams, maps, and mechanical drawings; all sorts of conventional signs; and so on"), the task of differentiating mediational means may seem relatively straightforward. As will become evident, however, identifying distinct psychological tools within natural language is somewhat more difficult.

Vygotsky addressed this to some extent in his account of speech functions, and here, as I have noted elsewhere (Wertsch, 1985c), he recognized at least four dichotomies: the signaling function versus the significative function, the social function versus the individual function, the communicative function versus the intellectual function, and the indicative function versus the symbolic function. The first three have to do with his general concern with the relationship between social and individual mental functioning, and the fourth is one version of the basic division he saw between semiotic potentials that lead to the emergence of inner speech and those that lead to the development of concepts.

Vygotsky's insights into various speech functions and his criteria for distinguishing them constitute a first step in identifying the various mediational means that make up a mediational tool kit. When we incorporate Bakhtin's ideas into the picture, however, it is possible to develop a much richer account, specifically, of how intermental and intramental processes are socioculturally situated. In this connection Bakhtin's notions of social language and speech genre are useful.

It might seem at first glance that Bakhtin's heavy emphasis on dialogic processes would preclude the identification of distinguishable forms of speech. He constantly returned to the idea that all speech involves some kind of interanimation of voices, thus excluding a neatly isolable, monologic perspective. One of Bakhtin's great accomplishments, however, was to specify forms of structure that organize dialogic processes. As I noted in Chapter 3, even though his focus was on utterances, he did not view "the individual language user to be an absolutely free agent with the ability to choose any words to implement a particular intention" (Holquist, 1986, p. xvi). Instead, he viewed social languages and speech genres as the means by which communicative and mental action are organized.

It is this that makes it possible to consider Bakhtin's ideas in light of the tool kit analogy. Although he did not formulate his thinking on social languages in these terms, there are grounds for making such a parallel in several of his statements. For example, "a speaker is given not only mandatory forms of the national language (lexical composition and grammatical structure), but also forms of utterances that are mandatory, that is, speech genres. The latter are just as necessary for mutual understanding as are forms of language. Speech genres are much more changeable, flexible, and plastic than [national] language forms are, but they have a normative significance for the speaking individuum, and they are not created by him but are given to him" (1986, pp. 80–81).

To identify some of the concrete problems that arise in considering various social languages and speech genres as items in a tool kit, it is useful to turn to someone who has formulated issues in this way. One figure whose ideas are instructive in this connection is Ludwig Wittgenstein. There are several interesting theoretical, and even historical, links between Wittgenstein, Bakhtin, and Vygotsky (Clark and Holquist, 1984; Toulmin, 1980). None of these links clearly indicates one author's direct influence on another. Instead, they suggest similarities and complementarities that seem to have arisen because of issues that were generally "in the air" at the time the three were writing. An essential point of similarity between Wittgenstein's ideas and those of Bakhtin can be found in Wittgenstein's notion of a "language game" and Bakhtin's notion of a social language. Both of these ideas, in turn, complement Vygotsky's concern with mediational means in that they highlight the multiplicity of mediational means (or psychological tools), although Vygotsky said little about this issue.

In *Philosophical Investigations*, Wittgenstein addressed the difficulty of distinguishing one language game from another and the issue of how language games could be conceptualized as being organized in a tool kit.

> Think of the tools in a tool-box: there is a hammer, pliers, a saw, a screw-driver, a rule, a glue-pot, nails and screws.—The functions of words are as diverse as the functions of these objects. (And in both cases there are similarities.)
>
> Of course, what confuses us is the uniform appearance of words when we hear them spoken or meet them in script and print. For their *application* is not presented to us so clearly. (1972, p. 6e)

Wittgenstein's comment that "what confuses us is the uniform appearance of words" is quite important. It is this insight that is so often

overlooked when we use the term "language" as if it refers to a homogeneous essence, when we speak of "language development" as if there
is a single, unified process, or when we engage in many other aspects
of theorizing about the role of speech and language. We need to
recognize the variety of uses to which language is put in human life.

Using another analogy, Wittgenstein elaborated on the problems
that arise from the misleading, homogeneous appearance of language.

> It is like looking into the cabin of a locomotive. We see handles all
> looking more or less alike. (Naturally, since they are all supposed to
> be handled.) But one is the handle of a crank which can be moved
> continuously (it regulates the opening of a valve); another is the
> handle of a switch, which has only two effective positions, it is either
> off or on; a third is the handle of a brake-lever, the harder one pulls
> on it, the harder it brakes; a fourth, the handle of a pump: it has an
> effect only so long as it is moved to and fro. (p. 7e)

In Bakhtinian terms, Wittgenstein's point translates into the claim
that it is often difficult to distinguish the various social languages and
speech genres in a national language. Even though different social
languages and speech genres serve different functions, they look "more
or less alike" in that they appear within a national language.

In this regard, some of Bakhtin's comments on the "social stratifica-
tion" of language (1981, p. 290) are quite suggestive. But his most
useful comments concern the utterance which he termed the *"real unit*
of speech communication" (1986, p. 71). According to Bakhtin, the
utterance has three fundamental properties: boundaries, finalization,
and generic form:

> regardless of how varied utterances may be in terms of their length,
> their content, and their compositional structure, they have common
> structural features as units of speech communication and, above all,
> quite clear-cut boundaries . . .
>   The boundaries of each concrete utterance as a unit of speech
> communication are determined by a *change of speaking subjects,* that
> is, a change of speakers. Any utterance—from a short (single-word)
> rejoinder in everyday dialogue to the large novel or scientific trea-
> tise—has, so to speak, an absolute beginning and an absolute end:
> its beginning is preceded by the utterances of others, and its end is
> followed by the responsive utterances of others (or, although it may
> be silent, others' active responsive understanding, or, finally, a re-
> sponsive action based on this understanding). The speaker ends his

utterance in order to relinquish the floor to the other or to make room for the other's active responsive understanding. The utterance is not a conventional unit, but a real unit, clearly delimited by the change of speaking subject, which ends by relinquishing the floor to the other, as if with a silent *dixi,* perceived by the listeners (as a sign) that the speaker has finished. (pp. 71–72)

As Bakhtin noted, the particular form this structural feature takes varies with different types of discourse: "This change of speaking subjects, which creates clear-cut boundaries of the utterance, varies in nature and acquires different forms in the heterogeneous spheres of human activity and life, depending on the functions of language and on the conditions and situations of communication" (p. 72). Among the types of utterance-rejoinder pairings he listed are "question and answer, assertion and objection, assertion and agreement, suggestion and acceptance, order and execution."

The second characteristic of the utterance as a unit of speech communication is its "finalization." This characteristic, which is "insepara-bly linked to the first," can be considered to be "the inner side of the change of speech subjects"; "This change [of speech subjects, or voices] can only take place because the speaker has said (or written) *everything* he wishes to say at a particular moment or under particular circumstances. When hearing or reading, we clearly sense the end of the utterance, as if we hear the speaker's concluding *dixi.* This finalization is specific and is determined by special criteria" (p. 76). The specificity of finalization in the last sentence means that different forms of finalization will characterize different social languages and speech genres, or spheres of human activity. In some cases (such as purely factual questions, requests, or orders), there is little room for variation and creativity in how an utterance can be finalized; in other cases, there is much greater latitude.

The third and "most important" characteristic of the utterance is its generic form. According to Bakhtin, the choice of a speech genre "is determined by the specific nature of the given sphere of speech communication, semantic (thematic) considerations, the concrete situation of the speech communication, the personal composition of its participants, and so on." As always, however, Bakhtin stressed that there are strict limits to how individuated an utterance can be: "When the speaker's speech plan with all its individuality and subjectivity is applied and adapted to a chosen genre, it is shaped and developed within a certain generic form" (p. 78).

In his discussion of the role of speech genres in shaping utterances, Bakhtin asserted that a major feature of the utterance is its relation "to the *speaker himself* (the author of the utterance) and to the *other* participants in speech communication." Under the first heading, he identified two subsidiary issues: 1) the fact that "each utterance is characterized primarily by a particular referentially semantic content," and 2) the fact that the "*expressive* aspect," or "the speaker's emotional evaluation of the referentially semantic content," must also be taken into account (p. 84).

The "referentially semantic content" refers to the topic of an utterance, and it is this that provides the focus of most accounts of speech. The referentially semantic content of an utterance might thus range from U.S. trade relations to the theory of relativity or a piece of a child's puzzle. Traditional semantic techniques in linguistics are concerned with related issues, but Bakhtin's focus on utterances rather than sentences or other sign types means that there is only limited overlap between the two kinds of approaches. Thus, because for Bakhtin an utterance is a link in the chain of speech communication, the referentially semantic content will depend on its place in relation to other utterances, whereas the referentially semantic content of a sentence is independent of such contextual factors.

The range of referentially semantic contents (or "spheres" or "themes") of utterances can be divided up according to several criteria. For example, it is possible to distinguish between objects that are assumed to exist independent of the utterance in the extralinguistic context and objects that are assumed to exist independent of the utterance but not in the immediate extralinguistic context. Thus, one can refer to a computer that is immediately present to perception as opposed to a computer that is not perceptually present but comes to be the object of interlocutors' attention because it is brought up in the conversation. The former case is grounded primarily in "extralinguistic indexical relationships," whereas the latter relies on "intralinguistic indexical relationships" (Wertsch, 1985c). The distinction between these two kinds of relationships, and the objects they involve, has been shown to be important for understanding various aspects of the development of language and thought. Hickmann (1985) and Karmiloff-Smith (1979), for example, have conducted extensive studies documenting the complex task of mastering anaphora (a type of intralinguistic indexical relationship), as I have already noted, and Wertsch and Minick (1990) have argued that anaphoric relationships are one of the basic building blocks of the "text-based realities" that characterize the discourse of formal instructional settings.

Another distinction one can use to delineate the kinds of referentially semantic contents available to speakers is that between nonlinguistic and linguistic objects. Under the linguistic heading are all those cases in which language is used to speak *about* language: one can speak about utterances as in reported speech, and one can speak about decontextualized relationships between sign types as in formal definitions. Vygotsky regarded this latter kind of reflective activity (using language to reflect on language) as a characteristic of formal instruction. This was his concern in examining the emergence of scientific concepts in adult-child discussion in this institutional setting. Following his lead, other investigators have made it the object of studies of related issues (Olson, 1977; Scribner, 1977; Wertsch and Minick, 1990).

The second issue Bakhtin considered under the heading of "the relation of the utterance to the *speaker himself* (the author of the utterance)" is the "*expressive* aspect." As he noted, this has traditionally been the province of stylistics. Although Bakhtin focused on the "speaker's subjective emotional evaluation" in his discussion of this issue, in a sociocultural approach to mediated action a more general notion of perspective, or point of view (Uspensky, 1973), on the referentially semantic content of an utterance is useful. This is consistent with Bakhtin's observation that "there can be no such thing as an absolutely neutral utterance" (1986, p. 84), but it admits of a wider set of issues—such as the "referential perspective" (Wertsch, 1980, 1985c), which plays such an important role in the dynamics of interpsychological functioning in the zone of proximal development—than were of interest to him.

Bakhtin's comments on "[the relation of the utterance] to the *other* participants in speech communication" form the core of his dialogically based account of the differences between the utterances of one social language and those of another. Whereas the referentially semantic content and the expressive aspect of utterances are properties that many theorists have used to characterize speech genres and other social languages, Bakhtin's major contribution was his understanding of how an utterance comes into contact with other utterances. Indeed, in his view, this form of dialogicality is present in almost every utterance: "utterances are not indifferent to one another and are not self-sufficient; they are aware of and mutually reflect one another." This awareness and reflection occur in many ways: "others' utterances can be repeated," "they can be referred to," "they can be silently presupposed," or "one's responsive reaction to them can be reflected only in the expression of one's own speech" (1986, p. 91).

It is not surprising that, given its central role in Bakhtin's thinking, dialogicality played a major role in his categorization of utterances, social languages, and speech genres. Examining the writings of Dostoevsky and others, he listed three major types and fourteen subtypes of "discourse with an orientation toward someone else's discourse (double-voiced discourse)." Among the subtypes are "parody with all its nuances," "any transmission of someone else's words with a shift in accent," "hidden internal polemic," "any discourse with a sideward glance at someone else's word," "a rejoinder of a dialogue," and "hidden dialogue" (1984, p. 199). Some of these categories (for example, parody, the transmission of someone else's words with a shift in accent, a hidden dialogue) have been relevant in the illustrations in Chapters 3 and 4, and all of them can be used in distinguishing one social language from another.

An Illustration

A Bakhtinian approach to meaning, especially as it touches on the criteria that distinguish among social languages and among speech genres, provides an essential means to address the issues of heterogeneity and the tool kit analogy. Given the novelty of this approach to meaning, I shall not attempt to provide a comprehensive, theoretically grounded typology of social languages or speech genres. Indeed, I shall not even try to generate a complete list of one class of items in a tool kit. Instead, I shall focus on a single speech genre, which arises in and struggles to play a dominant role in a specific sociocultural setting, that of formal schooling.

As we have seen, the criteria that distinguish one utterance from another are important in differentiating one speech genre from another. The boundaries of an utterance, its finalization, its referentially semantic content, its expressive aspect (perspective), and its relationship to other utterances are all useful criteria. The greater the level of detail of each of these criteria, the greater the number of speech genres that can be distinguished. Indeed, with enough detail, any utterance could probably be distinguished from all others. But following Bakhtin's emphasis on *types* of utterances when identifying speech genres, I shall refer to criteria that distinguish them at a more general level.

The particular speech genre I shall examine is used in classroom instruction in middle-class American elementary schools. One of its characteristics is a tendency toward certain kinds of classificatory schemes. This derives at least in part, as Bourdieu (1984) has noted, from the institutional framework within which formal instruction takes place: "in order to transmit at all, [the system of formal instruction] has to perform a degree of rationalization of what it transmits. Thus, for example, in place of practical schemes of classification, which are always partial and linked to practical contexts, it puts explicit, standardized taxonomies, fixed once and for all in the form of synoptic schemas or dualistic typologies (e.g., 'classical'/'romantic'), which are expressly inculcated and therefore conserved in the memory as knowledge that can be reproduced in virtually identical form by all the agents subjected to its action" (p. 67). In Vygotskian terms, scientific concepts emerge in formal instructional contexts at least in part because of the forces of rationalization (Habermas, 1970) that characterize human action in this institutional setting.

A further characteristic of this speech genre in formal instructional settings is a tendency which is opposed to that of the homogenization created by such rationality. In spite of the homogeneity of discourse that might be assumed to result from rationalization, on closer examination there is a diversity, or heterogeneity, even here. It is thus important not to be misled by "the uniform appearance of words," although the use of terms such as "classroom discourse," "teacher talk," and "the discourse of formal instruction" suggests just such homogeneity.

A major source of the heterogeneity I wish to examine is the difference between the voices of teachers and the voices of students: the former have mastered a fairly unified speech genre of formal instruction, whereas the latter have not. As a result, a certain type of heterogeneity emerges in the discourse of the classroom. Furthermore, even within the generally homogeneous speech genre used by teachers, there remains a great deal of heterogeneity. Different variants ("registers") of the general speech genre of formal instruction emerge in discourse with particular students and in connection with different subject matters.

A major reason for focusing on the sociocultural setting of formal instruction in an analysis of speech genres is that such settings are centrally concerned with socialization. Indeed, many of the social and psychological processes in formal instruction can be profitably viewed in terms of learning to speak the particular speech genres and "registers" of these languages and coming to understand the specific contexts in which variants should and should not be used.

The example of discourse I shall examine can be placed under the general heading of the "speech genre of formal instruction," and it is worth noting the general characteristics of this speech genre. The first of these is that there is a clear power difference between the voice of the teacher and the voices of the students. This is reflected in the fact that a large portion of the teacher's utterances are "directives" (Hickmann and Wertsch, 1978), which the students are expected to follow, whereas the students produce very few directives for the teacher. Directives need not be in the syntactic form of an imperative; in many instances they will be in interrogative or even declarative form. Their general function is to regulate students' mental processes (such as thinking or attention) in ways that are appropriate for the sociocultural setting of the classroom. The general reason for using so many of them is to provide a foundation of regulative utterances that can be mastered and internalized by the students themselves.

In this connection, consider a directive such as, "How many tens and how many ones are there in the top number?" When uttered by an elementary school teacher, this "instructional question" (Mehan, 1979) is hardly ever aimed at obtaining information; indeed, the hallmark of instructional questions is that the speaker obviously knows the answer. Instead, the aim of this directive is to help carry out the discourse needed to solve an arithmetic operation on the intermental plane. More specifically, it is a directive designed to get the student to participate in formulating the problem in the "right way." By responding to the directive, the student engages in a process sanctioned and regulated by the teacher.

Of course the ultimate aim of such directives is not to solve problems on the intermental plane. Teachers want to organize intermental functioning so that its patterns can be mastered and internalized by students; they want to foster the transition to intramental functioning. In this connection, a second property of the speech genre of formal instruction is that the teacher-student discourse is organized so that students are encouraged to take over more and more of the regulative responsibilities. As has often been noted about discourse concerned with the zone of proximal development, this involves a kind of negotiation between teacher and student (Wertsch, 1985c) in which teachers tend to use directives that require students to take on additional responsibility for regulating the activity. They constantly "test the waters" to see whether students can move to a new level of self-regulation. When students fail to meet these "semiotic challenges," teachers often return to using directives that require less on the part of the students, but this is usually followed by subsequent attempts to "up the ante" (Bruner, 1986) once again.

The specific register of the speech genre of formal instruction I shall examine here comes from a kindergarten classroom in an upper-middle-class school system in the suburbs of Chicago. The segment of discourse involves an activity setting known as "Show-and-Tell" time. In this setting, children, usually speaking individually before the group, make a short presentation about some experience or object from their life outside the classroom. It is a setting that is clearly set off, both by the explicit comments of the teacher ("Okay class, let's have Show-and-Tell time now"), and by the fact that children often move from desks or tables to an area on the floor where they all sit in a group.

In the following excerpt of discourse from this activity setting, the teacher is designated by T and various children are designated by C1, C2, and so forth.

(1) T: Danny (*C1*), please come up here with what you have. (*C1, with a piece of lava in his hand, approaches T.*)

(2) C2: I love (*unintelligible*).

(3) T: Marissa, we're waiting for you.

(4) C3: (*Addressed to C1*) Where did you get it?

(5) C1: From my mom. My mom went to the volcano and got it.

(6) T: And you know what? You were with her.

(7) C1: No I wasn't.

(8) T: Yes. You may have forgotten. I think you were just a little guy and you were sleeping. Mommy just told the story in the office that you were sleeping the day you went to Mount Vesuvius to get this lava rock. Isn't that something that . . . Is there anything you want to tell about it?

(9) C1: I've had it ever since I was . . . I've always . . .

(10) T: (*In a low voice to another child*) Careful.

(11) C1: I've always been, um, taking care of it.

(12) T: Uh hum.

(13) C1: It's never fallen down and broken.

(14) T: Uh hum. Okay. Is it rough or smooth?

(15) C1: Real rough and it's . . . and it's . . . and it's sharp.

(16) T: Okay. Why don't you go around and let the children touch it. Okay? (*C1 takes it around the group, which is sitting on the floor.*) Is it heavy or light?

(17) C1: It's heavy.

(18) T: It's heavy.

(19) C1: A little bit heavy.

(20) T: In fact, maybe they could touch it and hold it for a minute to see how heavy it is.

(21) C4: I didn't get a chance to hold it.

(22) T: And what do you have Lauren (C5)? You've got a . . .

(23) C5: Leather's holding this book.

(24) T: And what do you want us to find out in this?

(25) C5: There's something really neat.

(26) T: Yes?

(27) C5: (*Several children talking while C5 shows T something in the book*) . . . by your heart.

(28) T: By your heart?

(29) C5: Uh hum.

(30) T: Okay. You found something (*unintelligible*) heart. This one? Is that the picture you're interested in?

(31) C4: I'll hold.

(32) C5: Yeah.

(33) T: What does "heart" start with?

(34) C5: "H."

(35) T: "H." Okay. There she found in her dictionary a picture of the heart. And a picture of the veins and artery that lead to the heart, away from the heart. Okay. Did you find anything about volcanoes in here?

(36) C5: Uh. No.

(37) T: I'll bet there is under the sound for the letter "V." It's very possible. Let's see. Oh, look at this boys and girls . . . There is a volcano. It says, "an opening in the surface of the earth through which lava, gasses, and ashes are forced out. One of the most" . . . Danny . . . "one of the most active volcanoes is in Hawaii." Isn't that something? Now I wonder, should we look up lava?

(38) Several children: Yeah, yeah, yeah.

(39) T: Okay. We want lava. Yes?
(40) T: Okay. Wow. Wait till you hear what this says. It's something to do with (*unintelligible*). It says, "Lava is melted rock that comes out of a volcano when it erupts. It is rock formed by lava that has cooled and hardened. So that must have been hot lava that, that came out of the volcano. Once it cooled off, it got hard and, and now it's rock.
(41) C1: And it's . . . Know what? And it's still . . . it's still . . . Look . . . Shows from where it got . . . from where it was burned.

In this excerpt, there is a major difference between the ways that Danny (C1) and the teacher describe the object Danny has brought to Show-and-Tell. This difference, which will be analyzed in terms of "referential perspective" (Wertsch, 1980, 1985c), is highlighted in the teacher's use of instructional questions such as 14. The child formulates his utterances from the perspective of how the piece of lava is related to his individual life history (see utterances 5, 7, 9) and the personal characteristics of being careful and responsible (utterances 11, 13). Such a perspective is closely related to what Vygotsky's students and colleagues Luria (1981) and Leont'ev (1959) termed "sense"; in Bourdieu's terminology it is grounded in the "practical schemes of classification, which are always partial and linked to practical contexts" (1984, p. 67).

The teacher, in contrast, speaks of the object in quite different terms. After a couple of comments based on Danny's practical scheme of classification (utterances 6 and 8), she switches to a much different perspective. She poses instructional questions grounded in what Bourdieu identifies as "explicit, standardized taxonomies, fixed once and for all in the form of synoptic schemas." The categories she invokes even have the characteristics of "dualistic typologies" noted by Bourdieu (rough/smooth in utterance 14, and heavy/light in utterance 16). The reason for this taxonomic fixedness is that her categories are derived from sign type-sign type relationships, which are grounded in decontextualized mediational means (Wertsch, 1985c). Indeed, the prototype of such relationships—definitional equivalence relations as found in dictionaries—is what she turns to when she begins to use another child's dictionary in the latter part of the excerpt.

This teacher's use of the register of scientific concepts surfaces at many points and in many guises in teachers' classroom discourse.

Consulting a dictionary is not uncommon, but this register need not involve this practice. A major assumption made by those who use it is that meaning is ultimately grounded in closed, exhaustive systems of decontextualized sign type-sign type relationships, or "literal meanings." The linguistic ideology of literal meaning is often quite powerful, as reflected in the assumption that there is one "real" or "true" meaning of a word or expression and that this meaning can be defined in terms of its position in a system of decontextualized equivalence relationships.

Furthermore, and this is perhaps the most interesting point about the present example, the way teachers often organize classroom discourse reflects the assumption that this speech genre *should* be used to describe objects and events (Wertsch and Minick, 1990). Even if another form of description—or perspective—could be used to describe an object or event accurately and usefully in a particular problem setting, teachers send a strong implicit message that the speech genre of formal instruction is the appropriate one to use in this context. This is part of the classroom's system of "cognitive values" (Goodnow, 1990). The socialization procedures invoked in this case are instances of what Ochs (1988) has termed "indexical socialization" and involve the use of language to reflect and create specific contexts.

In the excerpt of classroom discourse above there is a kind of negotiation of meaning that is not uncommon in adult-child interaction of this sort: the teacher began by using Danny's perspective but quickly switched to the register of scientific concepts. Thus, she used the dichotomies of smooth/rough and heavy/light in order to reconceptualize or "recontextualize" the object in the framework of decontextualized mediational means. After she had described the object Danny had brought into the classroom in these terms, she switched again by consulting a dictionary, thereby moving into the realm of sign type-sign type relationships independent of any particular object. Definitions such as lava = "melted rock that comes out of a volcano when it erupts" are assumed to hold across all contexts and hence to be completely removed from any actual piece of lava. At this point she has moved another step away from Danny's original formulation; she is now using language to talk about linguistic, as opposed to extralinguistic, objects.

Finally, at the end of utterance 40 the teacher switches back to talking about the specific object (Danny's piece of lava), but now in terms of the scientific concepts she has introduced and elaborated with the help of the dictionary. One of the results of her discourse is that in utterance 41 Danny has followed the teacher's lead by switching from a description based in his life history and personality characteristics to one grounded in the scientific concepts introduced by the teacher; it is as if he has been persuaded that the correct, or at least appropriate, way to describe the object is in terms of its scientific properties.

The steps in the negotiation of perspective in this excerpt can be summarized as follows:

> *Phase 1* (utterances 5–13): Perspective of life history and personality characteristics. Piece of lava as referentially semantic content.
>
> *Phase 2* (utterances 14–20): Perspective of scientific concepts. Piece of lava as referentially semantic content.
>
> *Phase 3* (utterances 37–40): Perspective of scientific concepts. Other concepts as referentially semantic content.
>
> *Phase 4* (utterances 40–41): Perspective of scientific concepts. Piece of lava as referentially semantic content.

In this outline Phase 4 is a step back in the direction of Danny's original formulation in the sense that the teacher is at least talking about a nonlinguistic object. Yet it by no means reflects an acceptance of Danny's original formulation, since the object around which the discussion was originally organized has now been redefined through a shift in perspective. The negotiation of referential perspective in this case required more change on the part of the children than on the part of the teacher, something that correlates with the difference in power between the two interlocutors. The movement over the course of this segment of interaction has been one of children giving way to teacher: they have capitulated to her use of scientific concepts as an appropriate grounding for describing objects.

The view I have been outlining in this chapter suggests that the mediational means of human communicative and mental functioning can be usefully understood in terms of heterogeneity. This contrasts with the assumption that various forms of human activity rely on a single, undifferentiated form of mediation. In postulating heterogeneity, one immediately encounters the problem of how to formulate the relationship among the various mediational means or tools in the tool kit. I outlined three general sorts of relationships: heterogeneity as genetic hierarchy, heterogeneity despite genetic hierarchy, and nongenetic heterogeneity.

When the notion of heterogeneity is coupled with a Bakhtinian approach to meaning, I argued that speech genres are good candidates for the tools in the heterogeneous mediational tool kit (this was then extended to include registers of speech genres). This claim raised several additional questions, the first of which is how to distinguish one speech genre from another in some kind of principled way, and I turned to Bakhtin's account of the criteria for differentiating utterances (and hence for distinguishing one speech genre from another).

The illustration focused on discourse within the institution of formal instruction. The kind of heterogeneity involved was heterogeneity despite genetic hierarchy. Scientific concepts and instructional questions are used after children have already been using a variety of other forms of discourse, so that some sort of genetic hierarchy is involved. Furthermore, the appearance of these speech genres does not result in the disappearance of other speech genres. Children do not stop using perspectives grounded in everyday concepts and questions other than instructional questions after they master these forms of discourse. Heterogeneity is not therefore simply an issue of higher versus lower levels. Instead, an activity-oriented approach similar to Tulviste's (1988) is assumed to be appropriate here. Different speech genres are suited to different activity settings or spheres of life. By examining the use of different registers within a general sociocultural setting, it is possible to make quite detailed distinctions among such activity settings.

6

Sociocultural Setting, Social Languages, and Mediated Action

A t the outset, I stated that the goal of a sociocultural approach to mind is to explicate how human action is situated in cultural, historical, and institutional settings. As I have argued, the key to such an explication is the use of the notion of mediated action as a unit of analysis and the person(s)-acting-with-mediational-means as the relevant description of the agent of this action. From this perspective, any tendency to focus exclusively on the action, the person(s), or the mediational means in isolation is misleading. Yet the tendency to isolate various dimensions of a phenomenon is precisely what is encouraged by the disciplinary fragmentation that characterizes so much of the contemporary scholarship in the social sciences and humanities.

The claim that mediational means are inherently related to action is fundamental to the approach outlined here. Only by being part of action do mediational means come into being and play their role. They have no magical power in and of themselves. The widespread tendency in several disciplines to focus on language and other sign systems in isolation from their mediational potential usually means that one is not focusing on mediation at all but rather examining sign systems abstracted from human action. In the study of language, this focus undermines the notion that action and mediational means are mutually determining. It views the two sides of the coin as unrelated, and signs and sign systems as determining the structure of action in a mechanistic way. Furthermore, this focus on language systems in isolation is often associated with an emphasis on static structure, which obviously complicates attempts to account for genetic transition.

From the perspective of Vygotsky and Bakhtin, viewing mediational means in isolation from action is obviously misled. It would be criticized by Bakhtin (Voloshinov, 1973) for being grounded in the "abstract objectivism" often associated with the study of sentences as opposed to utterances, and it does not accord with Vygotsky's very definition of a sign (or "psychological tool") as "a means for psychologically influencing behavior" (1981a, p. 136).

In contrast, looking at action in isolation, without concern for the mediational means employed, loses sight of one of my most fundamental points and what is perhaps the most central contribution Vygotsky, Bakhtin, and many of their colleagues made to the study of mind: mediated action is an irreducible unit of analysis, and the person(s)-acting-with-mediational-means is the irreducible agent involved. The first of these points has been the topic of extensive debate among scholars concerned with Vygotsky's contribution to social science in the USSR. Georgi Shchedrovitskii (1981) has argued that A. N. Leont'ev's account of activity and action is flawed by the fact that Leont'ev lost sight of some of Vygotsky's insights about semiotic mediation.

With regard to the irreducibility of the person(s)-acting-with-mediational-means as the agent of action, the fact that western scientific and folk theories of mind are so steeped in the atomism and disengaged image of the self outlined by Taylor has resulted in a powerful tendency to lose sight of the role of socioculturally situated mediational means in shaping human action. Rather than accepting the person(s)-acting-with-mediational-means as an irreducible agent, there is a tendency to cast the individual acting in isolation in this role and to assume that any use of mediational means is ancillary or somehow based on some prior and independent individual intention.

By asserting that the agent of mental action cannot be reduced either to sign systems or to the individual in isolation, one challenges the assumption that processes and entities that have come to be isolated in various academic disciplines can be so neatly segregated. One raises questions, for example, about a great deal of contemporary scholarship in psychology, which has focused on the individual in isolation, and in linguistics, which has focused on sign systems in isolation.

The approach I have outlined also challenges the isolation imposed by other disciplinary boundaries. Their power is evident in the fact that in trying to create an approach critical of them, it is difficult to avoid terms that index their presence. This is reflected even here in my use of the terms *cultural, historical,* and *institutional* in speaking of sociocultural settings. These terms are intended to index the concerns of anthropology, history, and sociology, respectively, at least as these disciplines are currently understood in the United States.

The advantage of using these three terms is that they cover a range of phenomena generally understood by contemporary readers of social science literature. The problem with using them, of course, is that the tripartite division they involve introduces some of the very disciplinary fragmentation I am seeking to avoid. They encourage one to lose sight of the fact that there is no such thing as a purely cultural setting (one that has no historical or institutional dimensions) or a purely historical or purely institutional setting. Any setting obviously has cultural *and* historical *and* institutional aspects. What these three terms refer to are *dimensions,* or *ways of looking* at settings associated with disciplines, not some kind of fundamental essence of the settings themselves.

While many might agree with this point in principle, they might also argue that such distinctions are nonetheless useful for reasons of practicality: it is simply impossible to get research off the ground if one is asked to examine all the dimensions of a setting (cultural, historical, institutional, and psychological) simultaneously. As I remarked in Chapter 1, however, this kind of division of labor all too often leads to a collection of puzzle pieces that cannot be put back together again: the dimensions of a phenomenon are defined so that the constructs and units of analysis associated with each dimension are incompatible with one another and hence resistant to being recombined in a more comprehensive picture.

Making the Link between Mediated Action and Sociocultural Setting

As I have been arguing, the way out of the quandaries associated with disciplinary fragmentation is a fundamentally different type of unit of analysis, one that cuts across, or, better yet, ignores existing disciplinary lines. The ideal unit of analysis preserves in a microcosm (Vygotsky, 1987) as many dimensions of the general phenomenon under consideration as possible, thereby allowing one to move from one dimension to another without losing sight of how they fit together into a more complex whole. In short, I am suggesting not that specialized techniques and theoretical constructs are unnecessary but that in employing these techniques and constructs one should not use analytic dimensions that are guaranteed to remain isolated. There must always be a principled way to relate technical detail to other aspects of a general picture.

As I have argued, the way to achieve this desired end is through an appropriately formulated account of mediational means, and it was in this connection that I turned to the notions of dialogicality (especially ventriloquation), social language, and speech genre. These notions have made it possible not only to interrelate rather than segregate various aspects of the issues under discussion but also to delimit the object of analysis, that is, to create an object that does not put the investigator in the impossible position of having to provide a comprehensive analysis of everything before being able to take the first step. Bakhtin's ideas, as I have discussed them here, make it possible to examine concrete intermental and intramental functioning without losing sight of how this functioning is situated in historical, cultural, and institutional settings. Indeed, Bakhtin's views of social languages and speech genres and the dialogical processes by which they are appropriated almost guarantee the centrality of the relationship between psychological process and sociocultural setting.

The constructs I have outlined have proven useful in studies conducted from a variety of perspectives and thus might be considered as essential tools for interdisciplinary approaches seeking to understand the links between psychological process and sociocultural setting. Because of their general applicability they offer the possibility of drawing subdisciplines such as developmental psychology back into a more general social science discourse.

The wide relevance of claims about social languages and the tool kit analogy is illustrated in *Habits of the Heart: Individualism and Commitment in American Life* (Bellah et al., 1985). Although these researchers were not directly influenced by Bakhtin's ideas, the analytic tools they employed bear strong similarities to his notions of social language, voice, and ventriloquation. In analyzing their interview material, Bellah et al. relied heavily on the notion of the "cultural resources" interviewees use to make statements about how to "preserve or create a morally coherent life" (p. vii). They were concerned in particular with the variety of "voices" and "languages" used by their interviewees.

In defining their terms, Bellah et al. make an important distinction about "language": "We do not use *language* in this book to mean primarily what the linguist studies. We use the term to refer to modes of moral discourse that include distinct vocabularies and characteristic patterns of moral reasoning. We use *first language* to refer to the individualistic mode that is the dominant American form of discourse about moral, social, and political matters. We use the term *second languages* to refer to other forms, primarily biblical and republican, that provide at least part of the moral discourse of most Americans" (p. 334).

The parallels between this definition of "language" and Bakhtin's social language are striking. Not only do Bellah et al. distinguish their notion of language from that normally used in linguistics, but they associate it with particular categories of speakers, or voices. Furthermore, in stressing the ways in which the cultural resources of "languages" shape what people think and say, they rely on ideas about invoking or ventriloquating through a social language that are quite similar to those of Bakhtin. Finally, they envision a kind of dialogical interanimation among "languages" and voices reflected in some cases in the fact that one form is "dominant"; in others, they speak of the "several strands" of a cultural tradition and assert that cultural traditions are best understood as "arguments" or "dramatic conversations" (p. 27).

In formulating an account of "social science as public philosophy" Bellah et al. attempted to overcome the isolation of disciplinary fragmentation. They recognized the need to engage in "a conversation not only with those we interviewed but with representative figures of the various traditions, including the traditions of social science" (p. 306). Through their notion of "language," they created a vision encompassing several issues normally considered in isolation. For my purposes, the most important point about the notion of "language" in *Habits of the Heart* is that it enabled these researchers to avoid the segmentation and unidimensionality associated with studies that fall neatly within a single academic discipline. By grounding their analyses in "languages," they were able to examine those historical *and* cultural *and* institutional forces that shape ideas about a moral life in America and to do this *without* having to consider them in the kind of artificial isolation that precludes an integrated picture.

As a result, their study is difficult to classify. Although it has been categorized under sociology, moral philosophy, and several other disciplines, in the final analysis it encompasses them all. This is precisely its strength. By employing a construct very similar to Bakhtin's notion of social language, these researchers were able to develop a research focus that is "not psychological, or even primarily sociological, but rather cultural [in the broadest, nondisciplinary sense]" (p. x).

Privileging

In their account of "languages," Bellah et al. make two assumptions that are of fundamental interest for a sociocultural approach to mediated action. In a way consistent with the notion of heterogeneity, they assume that individuals have access to more than one "language," and they assume that these "languages" are organized in accordance with some kind of dominance hierarchy. Thus, they describe the language of individualism as "the dominant American form of discourse about moral, social, and political matters" (1985, p. 334), and they constantly refer to "first" and "second languages." In terms of the tool kit analogy, this again points to the notion that the items in the kit are organized in accordance with a hierarchy based on power or applicability.

I shall address the issue of the organization of mediational means in a dominance hierarchy in terms of the notion of "privileging." Privileging refers to the fact that one mediational means, such as a social language, is viewed as being more appropriate or efficacious than others in a particular sociocultural setting. My use of *privileging* instead of a term such as *dominant* or *domination* is motivated by several considerations. First, privileging comes with much less theoretical baggage attached to it, so one can use it in a more restricted sense. In addition, in contrast to domination, which is closely tied to the study of social structure, its focus is psychological processes. It is concerned with the fact that certain mediational means strike their users as being appropriate or even as the only possible alternative, when others are, in principle, imaginable.

Another reason for using privileging rather than domination is that the latter is often implicitly associated with some kind of stasis, whereas privileging is assumed to be more dynamic. It is dynamic in part because sociocultural settings do not mechanistically or unilaterally determine mediated action; in many settings it is at least possible for participants to define the situation in new, unexpected, or creative ways. Thus, there is a degree of dynamic negotiation involved. A major source of this dynamic derives from the fact that patterns of privileging are accessible to conscious reflection and hence, to self-generated change.

Often, only comparative analysis can confirm the fact that alternative mediational means might be used in a particular setting. The striking difference noted by Kearins (1981, 1986) in the way Australian white and aboriginal children approach a visual memory task is a case in point (see Chapter 2). Her findings indicate that subjects may differ over whether or not a task even requires verbal mediation.

In cases where it appears to be obvious that verbal mediation is required, there are often major differences in the social language and speech genre deemed appropriate. In such instances, the first response to a pattern of privileging quite different from one's own is often incredulity, as when one encounters texts from different cultures or historical periods. Taylor (1985b) has outlined such a case in his analysis of the emergence of scientific rationality in the West. In explicating this example he uses a notion of "language" that, as in the case of Bellah et al., bears a strong resemblance to the Bakhtinian idea of a social language: "The seventeenth-century revolution in scientific thought rejected previously dominant scientific languages in which what one can call an expressive dimension had an important part. This was the case, for instance, with the language of 'correspondences', in which elements in different domains of being could be thought to correspond to each other in virtue of embodying the same principle" (p. 141).

Taylor provides the following example from the writings of Francis Bacon as an illustration of how the "language of 'correspondences' " serves as a mediational means for "refuting" Galileo's discovery of the moons of Jupiter.

> There are seven windows given to animals in the domicile of the head, through which the air is admitted to the tabernacle of the body, to enlighten, to warm, and to nourish it. What are these parts of the microcosmos: Two nostrils, two eyes, two ears and a mouth. So in the heavens, as in a macrocosmos, there are two favourable stars, two unpropitious, two luminaries, and Mercury undecided and indifferent. From this and from many other similarities in nature, such as the seven metals, etc., which it were tedious to enumerate, we gather that the number of planets is necessarily seven. (p. 141)

Taylor's remark that "the argument seems ludicrous to us today" serves as a comment about the pattern of privileging found in two different sociocultural settings. This is not to say that outside interference in the form of institutionally imposed sanctions is not involved. The institutional powers of today, like those of the seventeenth century, have a vested interest in seeing one "language" used rather than another, and a sociocultural approach readily recognizes this. At the same time, Taylor's comment also acknowledges that the psychological process of privileging is another legitimate moment in the overall picture.

Examples such as this, which can easily be multiplied in other historical and anthropological writings, clarify the issue. It is not as simple as having or not having a mediational means like the rational language that pervades modern scientific discourse. If this were the case, one might expect modern readers to experience difficulty in merely understanding the passage from Bacon. The problem is one of believing that anyone would want to appropriate a social language like Bacon's in order to deal with the structure of the solar system.

The Bacon example is a further reminder that mediational means are often used with little or no conscious reflection. Indeed, it is often only when confronted with a comparative example that one becomes aware of an imaginable alternative. This conscious awareness is one of the most powerful tools available for recognizing and changing forms of mediation that have unintended and often untoward consequences. In some cases, such as that of the QWERTY keyboard described in Chapter 2, it is relatively easy to demonstrate the deficiencies in a particular mediational means. In others, however, the process of recognizing, let alone changing, a pattern of privileging is much more complex, given the extreme difficulty in characterizing and consciously reflecting on the social languages in a mediational tool kit.

This focus on privileging by no means obviates the need to consider the outside interference outlined by Taylor in his critique of atomism and the disengaged image of the self. But such outside interference now occurs in a kind of self-imposed way. In place of externally imposed sanctions and other social processes, including those of external interference, which influence the development of a pattern of employing mediational means, privileging takes on an essentially psychological dimension for those who employ these means.

In accordance with ideas outlined in the preceding chapters, I shall examine privileging by looking at the genetic processes through which speakers come to master social languages. A fundamental dynamic in the four illustrations that follow is the transition from intermental to intramental functioning. Thus it involves the "primordial dialogue of discourse" outlined by Bakhtin. But the notions of social language, speech genre, and ventriloquation provide a foundation for recognizing how other categories of dialogicality are also involved. Of particular concern is the fact that in interacting with another concrete voice, the children in the illustrations are also simultaneously interacting with, and appropriating, generalized voice types, that is, social languages and speech genres. One of the fundamental processes of development, therefore, is mastering the process of ventriloquating through various social languages and speech genres.

In approaching these illustrations the Bakhtinian question "Who is doing the talking?" will always be at the core of the inquiry, and the investigator must constantly listen for at least two voices in formulating an answer. In order to disentangle the voices and social languages involved, I shall turn to the criteria for characterizing utterances outlined by Bakhtin (see Chapter 5), particularly those concerned with referentially semantic content, the speaker's relationship to the utterance, and the speaker's relationship to the utterances of others. These criteria will not generate a short, neat list of social languages or speech genres. There are so many ways that a speech genre or social language, or a register of either, may differ from others that it is more reasonable to expect a long, often disorganized, and constantly changing list.

The illustrations will again be concerned with action that takes place in a particular sociocultural setting—formal schooling. In some cases I shall use excerpts of classroom discourse from observational studies and in others empirical findings from more controlled studies. As I noted in the Show-and-Tell illustration in Chapter 5, classroom discourse, especially while it is being mastered by students, is not a monolithic essence. Instead, it involves several registers of social languages and speech genres.

The Place of "Noninstructional Experience Statements"

In mastering classroom discourse one must focus on a circumscribed set of objects, experiences, and topics, which provide the appropriate range of the referentially semantic content of the social language. An underlying assumption of most sessions of formal instruction is that one must not introduce or presuppose information from "outside" the classroom unless specifically invited to do so. It is as if an invisible barrier has been placed around the topical "space" that is eligible for discussion.

The power of this assumption about "outside information" is

reflected in the fact that those activities in which it is not in force are explicitly separated off from others. In the Show-and-Tell example in Chapter 5, the activity was marked off by physical location, by the introductory and concluding comments of the teacher (see also Michaels, 1981), and by its focus on a referentially semantic content that is not usually acceptable in formal instructional settings. Students were invited to talk about objects and events outside the realm of classroom activity. As the illustration clearly showed, however, even in this setting there is a tendency for the teacher to redirect the discourse back to the referentially semantic content more typical of formal instructional settings.

The types of utterances that typically distinguish Show-and-Tell time from other kinds of classroom discourse constitute what I shall term "noninstructional experience statements." These are utterances whose referentially semantic content does not fall within the topics appropriate for formal instruction. Their use indicates a shift to a speech genre distinct from that which predominates in formal instructional activities.

Three principal criteria distinguish the referentially semantic content of noninstructional experience statements from other aspects of formal instructional discourse. First, they refer to experiences and events that occur outside the classroom. They contrast with utterances directly concerned with the formal instructional setting (Teacher: "Why do you think the boy in the story we just read was afraid of the dog?"), and those concerned with "classroom management" (Child: "Bryan won't let me sit in this chair"; Teacher: "Go find another chair then"). Second, they are concerned with experience or knowledge to which the speaker has privileged access, rather than with experience or knowledge grounded in the shared experiential background provided by the classroom. This property is similar to one Bernstein (1975) has used to characterize "restricted codes," although this similarity should not be taken to suggest that noninstructional experience statements and restricted codes are the same. Bernstein's dichotomy of "restricted" and "elaborated" codes is based on the assumption that it is possible to demarcate a few, generally describable types of speech. This assumption contrasts with the multiplicity of social languages and speech genres suggested by Bakhtin's approach. The third property of noninstructional experience statements is that they are not responses to utterances motivated by the needs of an instructional activity (a teacher's question, "Do any of you have a dog at home?" at the beginning of a reading exercise about dogs).

On occasion, noninstructional experience statements occur in classroom discourse in situations other than Show-and-Tell time. These occurrences are of particular interest in understanding the developing mastery of a tool kit of social languages and speech genres in this sociocultural setting. For example, the following utterance was made by a first-grade student in a middle-class American classroom to her teacher:

(1) My brother got his braces out.

This utterance was embedded in the flow of activity surrounding an arithmetic problem. The teacher replied,

(2) He did? That's wonderful. Now how did you do this last problem?

The teacher's response is quite typical. In such cases the teacher acknowledges the student's utterance but in a way that discourages further utterances on the topic. The student's statement is treated as an irrelevant digression or an inappropriate switch in register.

A striking fact about students' noninstruction experience statements is that they seem to occur infrequently in elementary school classrooms, even during quite early phases of schooling. In an analysis of videotapes of six full days of interaction in a first-grade classroom, Hagstrom and Wertsch (in preparation) found only twelve instances of noninstructional experience statements by students. Three of these days involved a teacher who is generally viewed as quite orderly and strict in her approach to classroom control, and the other three involved a teacher whose classroom would be judged to be much more "open" in style. Noninstructional experience statements occurred so infrequently that meaningful comparisons are difficult to make, but it is noteworthy that all such statements did not occur in the more open classroom.

In a related observation, more than half of the noninstructional experience statements occurred immediately after an activity involving a social language in which they would have been appropriate. For example, utterance 1 occurred just after the classroom had made the transition from a kind of Show-and-Tell time to regular instruction. Children had just been making utterances in one speech genre when the activity setting changed and another speech genre was deemed appropriate. Some children apparently had difficulty recognizing the change or were unable to switch from one register to another as easily and completely as the change in activity setting demanded. In a sense, they had mastered several aspects of the various speech genres involved, but they had not gained adequate facility and flexibility in the changing patterns of privileging required in the classroom.

In terms of the Bakhtinian question, "Who is doing the talking?" it is obvious that the first graders in the two classrooms examined by Hagstrom and Wertsch had already been extensively socialized into ventriloquating through a speech genre appropriate for that particular sociocultural setting. In an essential sense, of course, individual students continue to speak; this is reflected in the fact that each student is generally considered to be responsible for what he or she says and not for the utterances of others. But the closely circumscribed range of referential semantic content in the students' utterances in the classroom reveals that they have come to privilege a specific speech genre in producing their utterances. Through a process of ventriloquation, a specific type of socioculturally situated voice can be heard alongside the individual child's voice.

Of course, by being socialized away from using noninstructional experience statements in specific activity settings in the classroom, children are not being socialized away from using them in general. Speech genres grounded in such utterances continue to be part of children's tool kit of mediational means regardless of how successful they are at ventriloquating through a social language in the classroom. This is immediately apparent in the dialogues between teachers and students during recess or in other noninstructional settings. Here, the discourse is full of noninstructional experience statements, at least on the part of students, and they are often encouraged by the teacher's response. The process of socialization is obviously not one of replacing one speech genre with another; instead it is one of differentiating and adding speech genres. It is a case of heterogeneity despite genetic hierarchy. Furthermore, socialization involves mastering the rules for using particular speech genres in particular sociocultural settings.

The Categorization of Nonlinguistic and Linguistic Objects

As I noted in Chapter 3, Vygotsky's account of conceptual development was undergoing a major shift near the end of his life, one that was clearly reflected in the fifth and sixth chapters of *Thinking and Speech* (1987). As he moved away from analyzing conceptual development primarily from the perspective of intramental functioning and toward focusing on the role of intermental functioning, his position shifted toward the view that mastery of scientific concepts is fundamentally linked with participation in discourse of a particular type, namely, formal instructional discourse in classrooms.

As Minick (in press; also see Wertsch and Minick, 1990) and others have argued, scientific conceptual discourse takes on many guises in formal instruction settings. I shall focus on one specific type here, utterances concerned with relationships between sign types (Wertsch, 1985c), which is a primary focus in Vygotsky's approach to the development of word meaning. An essential aspect of the emergence of this kind of utterance is that it involves a new category of object, specifically, a linguistic object. In addition to using language to represent nonlinguistic reality, a new reality in the form of decontextualized sign types can now be represented and operated on. In Bakhtinian terms, this means that a new kind of referentially semantic content and hence, a new speech genre are at issue. Furthermore, this kind of utterance creates new possibilities for patterns of privileging.

The difference between "everyday" and scientific concepts involved here concerned Luria (1976a) in his study of "practical," or "situational," reasoning on the one hand and "theoretical" reasoning on the other, and it has concerned a variety of other investigators, many of whom have been influenced by Luria's pioneering work (Cole and Scribner, 1974; Scribner, 1977). One of the basic procedures employed in such research is to ask subjects to categorize sets of objects (often pictures of objects). For example, subjects may be shown drawings of a hammer, a saw, a hatchet, and a log and asked to state which one does not belong or which three go together. The basic finding reported by Luria is that subjects who had had no schooling refused or were unable to categorize objects in ways generally recognized as "correct" by subjects who had had even a few months of schooling. The nonschooled subjects tended to assume that the items to be categorized were the nonlinguistic objects represented by the terms involved. As a result, they grouped items on the basis of how the nonlinguistic objects identified by the pictures function in a practical situation. In contrast, schooled subjects tended to assume that the objects to be categorized were the decontextualized word meanings associated with the pictures. As a result, they grouped items on the basis of decontextualized semantic relationships such as synonymy and hyponymy.

An example of the first type of categorization (Luria's "practical" or "situational" reasoning) is the response of a thirty-nine-year-old nonschooled peasant from a rural area in Soviet Central Asia to Luria's question about which three of the four items (hammer, saw, hatchet, log) go together. This subject responded that all four objects were needed. When presented with the fact that someone else had said that the hammer, saw, and hatchet go together, the subject responded that the other person probably used that grouping because "he's got a lot of firewood, but if we'll be left without firewood, we won't be able to do anything." When pressed further by Luria with the observation that the hammer, saw, and hatchet can all be labeled by the same term, the subject responded, "Yes, but even if we have tools, we still need wood—otherwise, we can't build anything."

The basic difference between experimenter and subject in this session arose because the former was trying to categorize linguistic objects (decontextualized word meanings), whereas the latter was categorizing the nonlinguistic referents of terms. The reason that Luria viewed hammer, saw, and hatchet as going together was that the *word meanings* all fall under, or are hyponyms of, the more general term *tool*. The semantic relationship of hyponymy involved here exists quite independent of the concrete objects the terms may be used to designate. Indeed, such abstract sign type-sign type relationships can be created and operated upon even if one has never had direct experience with the objects designated by the words.

Experience in certain kinds of formal instructional settings seems to be a crucial determinant of a subject's willingness and ability to focus on abstract linguistic objects. Scribner and Cole (1981) have argued that the "literacy practice" characteristic of the instructional settings one encounters in formal schooling in the West is the crucial factor. In the terminology I have used here, this means that a certain speech genre must be used extensively and mastered and that it will tend to be privileged, at least in certain settings.

As an example of the kind of socialization experience that produces this pattern of privileging, consider the following segment of classroom interaction. This segment involves an experienced teacher interacting with a group of six students in her first-grade classroom. The school involved is in a middle-class suburb of Chicago, and it had been in session for slightly over two months at the time this episode occurred.

(1) T: Okay. Let's turn over . . . This is fun. There's one picture in every row that does *not* belong. Which one doesn't belong in the first one? John, what doesn't belong?

(2) C: Key.

(3) T: Key. Put an X on the key. Why doesn't the key belong Mikey?

(4) C: Umm . . . They can't open doors.

(5) T: Oh . . . That's not a good answer. Why doesn't the key belong with the ham and a tomato and a banana, Mikey?

(6) C: Because the key isn't a fruit.

(7) T: Well, a ham isn't a fruit. What are all those things? Things you can . . .

(8) C: Eat.

(9) T: Eat. Things you can eat. You can eat a ham. You can eat a tomato. You can eat a banana. Can you eat a key?

(10) C: No.

(11) T: No. So cross it off. Okay, now do the next one. Let's take a look. Which one are we going to put an X on, Jessica?

(12) C: The plant.

(13) T: The plant. Why? Annie.

(14) C: Because it's not clothes.

(15) T: It's not clothes. Good. All the rest are clothes. Okay, how about the next one? What are you going to put an X on, Fuad?

(16) C: Umm. Apple.

(17) T: Why?

(18) C: It's not a tool.

(19) T: It's not a tool. Patrick, which one are you going to *eliminate* in the last one?

(20) C: Umm . . . The goose.

(21) T: Why?

(22) C: Because it's not something you can sit on or sleep on.

(23) T: Very good. It's not furniture, right? We can call that furniture.

Several things about these interchanges are quite striking. The first is the clearly negative response (utterance 5) the teacher gave to

Mikey's answer. More relevant to the issue of how one speech genre comes to be privileged over others is the reason behind the teacher's dismissal of Mikey's answer. Mikey identified the correct item to be eliminated from the group, but he invoked the wrong criteria for making, or at least for justifying, his selection. Instead of justifying his choice on the basis of sign type-sign type relationships (how the linguistic objects are organized in a semantic hierarchy), he justified it on the basis of how the nonlinguistic objects designated by the pictures may or may not be used in similar ways.

In formulating his answer, Mikey had appropriated a speech genre which assumes that the function of the pictures is to depict nonlinguistic objects. The teacher was operating in a speech genre which assumes that the pictures serve to index decontextualized semantic terms, a kind of linguistic object. Mikey seems to have recognized this immediately and provided an answer based on decontextualized semantic relations in 6. In this case, his answer was still wrong, but at least it was grounded in the speech genre deemed appropriate for the setting by the teacher.

During the course of this interaction the teacher often switched back and forth between the two kinds of referentially semantic content and hence between the two speech genres involved. After apparently trying to elicit a superordinate term ("food" in utterance 7), she switched to talking about the function of the nonlinguistic objects themselves. Instead of focusing on the fact that the terms *ham, banana,* and *tomato* are all subordinate to the term *food,* she focused on the functional similarity of the nonlinguistic objects (they are all objects one can eat).

In the following interchange (utterances 11 to 15), Jessica invoked the appropriate speech genre to justify her answer, and the teacher responded positively. This was also true of the next interchange involving Fuad (utterances 15 to 19). Finally, in the interchange between the teacher and Patrick (utterances 19 to 23), the student selected the correct item, but he did not appropriate the correct speech genre in doing so. As a result, the teacher "translated" his response from one grounded in action with nonlinguistic objects to one grounded in abstract semantic relations.

The differences between the two speech genres are quite difficult to detect, because there is no surface marking in oral speech to distinguish between using sign tokens (actual occurrences of terms such as *key*) to refer to nonlinguistic objects and using sign tokens to refer to linguistic objects (in this case, decontextualized word meanings). In fact, the shift in Mikey's answer (from utterance 4 to utterance 6) indicates that he recognized this difference in speech genres, but without the metalinguistic terminology of "sign tokens," "sign types," and so forth, it is extremely difficult for him or for the analyst to be explicit about such distinctions. Given this difficulty, it is perhaps surprising that students are ever able to recognize, let alone master, the formal instructional speech genres grounded in decontextualized word meanings.

The Power of Persuasion and the Speech Genres of Official Science

The first two illustrations relied primarily on referentially semantic content to delineate aspects of speech genres. The next illustration focuses on how a speaker's utterance relates to the utterances of others in a relationship of power, but in this case I will be concerned with the students' rather than the teacher's voice.

As we have seen, the notion of privileging is concerned with the psychological aspect of judging which social languages and speech genres are more appropriate than others in a particular sociocultural setting. During the process of mastering patterns of privileging, this judgment may rely heavily on the guidance of others that is provided through intermental functioning. This was a major factor in the cases thus far. What begins as external interference on the intermental plane, however, is gradually transformed to a kind of self-imposed interference, an intramental process. In this connection, we come to feel that some social languages and speech genres are more appropriate than others for describing and explaining various phenomena. Conversely, as Taylor makes clear in his account of Bacon's response to Galileo, the use of some social languages in a particular setting may be viewed as inappropriate or even "ludicrous."

One kind of speech genre that is widely judged to be more appropriate than others in the sociocultural setting of formal instruction is what I shall term the speech genre of "official science." The official science at issue here is the science explicitly taught in the formal curriculum. Since there are many topics covered in science curricula and since there are many stages in the mastery of each, no single, monolithic speech genre of official science can be defined. The property that unifies them is the fact that they are grounded in the science curriculum.

There has recently been a great deal of research on the mastery of the concepts of "official science" (Wiser, 1988; Hatano and Inagaki, in press). Much of the debate generated by this research has revolved around how the concepts children seem to generate spontaneously to describe and explain various phenomena are related to the concepts of official science. Some investigators have argued that the concepts of official science grow naturally out of everyday concepts universally developed by children, whereas others have argued that the emergence of the concepts of official science involves a qualitative shift in development.

The notion of privileging is not tied directly to either of these approaches, but it is more compatible with the latter in that it always presupposes the kind of heterogeneity suggested by qualitative shifts. In terms of the development of scientific concepts, it is compatible with the notion of heterogeneity despite genetic hierarchy suggested by Giyoo Hatano and Kayoko Inagaki (in press). Although they have not formulated their findings in terms of speech genres, privileging, and heterogeneity, Hatano and Inagaki have dealt with several of the issues under discussion here. They have conducted extensive analyses of children's developing understanding of scientific knowledge and have noted that even when elementary school children clearly have access to the kind of concepts and reasoning procedures taught in the science curriculum (that is, to the social language of official science), they often employ everyday concepts, in particular, in settings where they are asked to function individually (on the intramental plane). The researchers take this as evidence that at least at a certain point in development students have more trust or faith in these concepts than they do in those provided by official science.

The sociocultural situatedness of this kind of judgment comes into focus if one considers students' judgments in settings where the speech genre of official science clearly has positive status. As an example of how privileging occurs in such a setting and the "power of persuasion" that is attached to it, I shall outline an illustration from a classroom interaction that occurred in accordance with the Hypothesis-Experiment-Instruction Method studied by Hatano and his colleagues (Hatano and Inagaki, in press). In this procedure, students are presented with an experimental apparatus and asked to predict the outcome of some operation on it. Before being allowed to carry out or witness the operation, students are asked to engage in a debate among themselves about the expected outcome. Typically, the students vote publicly in favor of their own prediction and try to persuade those who disagree to change their minds.

The particular apparatus at issue have consisted of a ball of Plasticine clay two inches in diameter suspended from a fixed frame by a spring six inches in length. The students were asked what would happen to the length of the spring when the ball of clay was placed in a cup of water. Would the spring: a) get longer; b) get shorter; or c) stay the same? The students in this case were from a public school in the Boston, Massachusetts, area. Their classroom was a combined third- and fourth-grade room taught by an experienced teacher.

My analysis here will focus on one segment of a particular discussion involving Ian, a fourth-grade child. In the session at issue many of the students had participated in the discussion and some had changed their votes before Ian spoke. At this point, he argued for the view that the spring would become longer.

Ian: How, how, if it's at that height, I don't see why the water would make it sink.

Sam: (*Interrupts*) I know because, something's holding it.

Ian: (*Continuing*) Even if it's held up, even if you put space around it, it would go up. I mean, it's a different atmosphere for changing. I mean, you could put lava around it, or fire around it, it wouldn't do anything.

Adults, even those with a very limited knowledge of official science, are likely to be amused by Ian's comments. Although his "explanation" has very little to do with the relevant physical processes at issue it seems to have had a powerful effect on the rest of the students. To some degree this effect was reflected in the discussion that ensued, but it is most clearly manifested in findings from follow-up interviews. In interviews with eleven out of twenty-two students who had participated in the debate, five mentioned that Ian's comments were smart. Justin, for example, said that "Ian had a really good comment. I just remembered that I kind of, I understood it and said, 'Now that's a pretty good idea.' " Some of their comments indicate that Ian's persuasiveness may have stemmed from his general reputation as intelligent in academic matters.

It is essential to recognize, however, that Ian did not simply cast a vote for one of the three options and let his reputation serve to persuade his classmates. He formulated an argument to support his opinion, and there was something in that argument that seems to have been as instrumental as Ian's general reputation in convincing the other children. Several of them commented that there was something about what Ian said that was "good." A key aspect of Ian's persuasiveness seems to have been his appropriation of fragments, such as vocabulary, from the speech genre of official science. His use of *atmosphere, lava,* and *fire* is particularly noteworthy in this respect, especially since no other child invoked such terms.

In terms of a Bakhtinian approach to meaning (see Chapter 4), the relevant question here once again is "Who is doing the talking?" The answer is that more than one voice is involved. One the one hand, Ian produced the words, so his individual voice is involved. On the other, he ventriloquated through what he understood to be the speech genre of official science. Like any speech genre, this one is characteristic of certain sociocultural settings and belongs to other speakers who have used it. As a result, these other voices are evident in Ian's utterances. Therefore, regardless of how inadequate Ian's understanding and appropriation of this speech genre are, his utterances are multivoiced in a specific way.

In appropriating certain aspects of the meaning system of this speech genre, Ian appropriated certain aspects of its power. Inherent in this view of the issue is the assumption that power and status apply neither to the individual nor to the speech genre in isolation. As already noted, the other children pointed to what Ian *said* when describing why they were persuaded by his comments; they did not seem to be convinced simply because Ian was doing the talking. Conversely, the speech genre considered in isolation does not confer automatic power or status on those who appropriate it. One has no difficulty imagining situations in which other children's attempts to ventriloquate through this speech genre would be met with incredulity and amusement in place of the respectful reception Ian's appropriation met. All this is consistent with the claim that the agent involved is the person-acting-with-mediational-means.

Returning to the process of privileging, it is important to note that many of the children were persuaded by Ian's comments even though these were, in actuality, misguided and largely irrelevant to the physical phenomenon at hand. Ian's classmates had begun to believe that in formal instructional settings the speech genres of official science have some kind of explanatory power superior to their own ideas. This is not to say that they "really" believed something else and were simply acquiescing to another opinion under threat of some kind of social sanction. The reflections they provided on why they thought the spring would get longer or shorter indicate that they accepted the superiority of this speech genre in a more basic sense.

"Reciprocal Teaching" and the Dialogic Structure of Sociocultural Settings

The illustrations thus far have been concerned with describing how meaning is generated and transformed in formal instructional settings. In a final example, I shall turn to an illustration of how researchers and practitioners have harnessed processes of dialogicality to *change* these settings. This case concerns the procedure of "reciprocal teaching" devised by A. S. Palincsar and A. L. Brown (1984, 1988). In this procedure, students are specifically required to lead a dialogue (that is, pose questions usually reserved for the teacher) in a task setting. Instead of mastering the process of asking the right questions through experience in responding to them, instruction is organized in a more direct manner; children explicitly voice the questions themselves.

Palincsar and Brown have applied this procedure primarily to the psychological processes involved in reading comprehension. They have focused in particular on "the active strategies the reader employs to enhance understanding and retention, and to circumvent comprehension failures." As they note, extensive research has shown that these strategies, in conjunction with "facility with decoding," "considerate texts," and "the compatibility of the reader's knowledge and text content" (1984, p. 118) are the major determinants of reading comprehension.

After reviewing the major functions that must be carried out for reading to be successful, Palincsar and Brown identified four concrete activities in which to engage students as they attempt to learn the strategies of comprehension skills: *summarizing* (self-review), *questioning*, *clarifying*, and *predicting*. Noting that these are precisely the kinds of activities that poor readers do not carry out, Palincsar and Brown devised a set of training and assessment procedures for students at various grade levels who had been identified as having major problems in developing reading skills. The core of these procedures revolved around reciprocal teaching, in which students and teachers take turns leading the discussion of texts, generating summaries and predictions, and clarifying misleading or complex sections of the text.

Palincsar and Brown note that the poor readers in a pilot study they conducted with seventh graders initially "had great difficulty assuming the role of dialogue leader when their turn came." As a result, "the adult teacher was sometimes forced to construct paraphrases and questions for the students to mimic." This procedure would at first glance seem to be of questionable utility, since, as Palincsar and Brown themselves admit, "the students were relatively passive observers" (p. 125) in such a process. But according to the procedures of reciprocal teaching, students are not allowed to remain in this passive role. They are encouraged to take on an increasingly active responsibility for the strategic processes involved in reading comprehension.

The procedure of reciprocal teaching has produced some interesting results. Palincsar and Brown report that at the end of a relatively small number of sessions, poor readers show remarkable improvement in making the transition from being directed by the teacher to operating independently: "Gradually, the students became much more capable of assuming their role as dialogue leader and by the end of ten sessions were providing paraphrases and questions of some sophistication. For example, in the initial sessions half of the questions produced by the students were judged as nonquestions or as needing clarification; however, by the end of the sessions, unclear questions had dropped out and were replaced with questions focusing on the main idea of each text segment. A similar improvement was found for summary statements. At the beginning of the sessions, only a few summary statements captured main ideas, whereas at the end, the majority of the statements were so classified" (p. 125).

Furthermore, student improvement was by no means limited to performance in the reciprocal teaching sessions: "Each day, before (baseline), during, and after (maintenance) training, the students took an unassisted assessment, where they read a novel passage and answered ten comprehension questions on it from memory. From their baseline performance of 15% correct, they improved during training to accuracy levels of 85%, levels they maintained when the intervention was terminated. Even after a 6-month delay, the students averaged 60% correct without help, and it took only 1 day of renewed reciprocal teaching to return them to the 85% level achieved during training" (p. 125). These results are vastly superior to those normally achieved in training studies with poor readers. Numerous studies and treatment procedures have had little success in improving students' performance during the instruction sessions, and maintenance has been much rarer still.

Although not explicitly motivated by the Bakhtinian concerns I have described, the procedure of reciprocal teaching devised by Palincsar and Brown has strong parallels with several of Bakhtin's fundamental tenets. For example, notions about internalizing the dialogic structure of this procedure surface at several points in their account, something that is not all that surprising, given that the authors formulate their approach partly in terms of Vygotsky's ideas. In outlining the relationship between students' improved performance in the intermental processes of reciprocal teaching and their performance on the unassisted assessment, they note, "these scores [on unassisted assessment measures] were obtained on *privately read* assessment passages, that is, different texts that the students read independently after their interaction with the instructor. What was learned during the instructional sequence was used independently by the learners" (p. 125). In terms of the constructs I have been using, this means that a kind of external interference has been transformed into a self-imposed, intramental process.

The nature of the speech genres involved and their interanimation is particularly interesting in this connection. The speech genre of formal instruction is perhaps most clearly manifested in the instructional questions the students were encouraged to use. As in the case of all instructional questions, those posed by students in reciprocal teaching do not function to elicit information the speaker does not have. For example, the question, "Where does lightning get its charge?" (Palincsar and Brown, 1984, p. 136), posed after the interlocutors had read a passage about lightning, is not a genuine request for information. Instead, it functions to direct attention in ways that are relevant to the processing strategies deemed appropriate in this setting. Underlying the use of such questions is an essential assumption about the relationship between the utterances of the speakers and the other students, namely that the speaker has the right to ask such questions and the interlocutors have the responsibility to answer them. This right is normally the teacher's, but in reciprocal teaching, students are asked to appropriate it along with other aspects of the speech genre normally reserved for the teacher.

By making the switch from having students respond to teachers' utterances (the normal instructional format) to requiring students to formulate their own questions and directives, Palincsar and Brown have effected a fundamental shift in the arrangement of voices that ventriloquate through the speech genre of formal instruction. The procedure they have employed uses a form of explicit ventriloquation in which students are asked to mimic the form of the teacher's utterances even before they understand essential aspects of its meaning. This contrasts with the assumption that students will automatically come to appropriate instructional questions by being exposed to them in the speech of others (especially teachers).

As an example of the explicit ventriloquation involved in reciprocal teaching, here is an interaction between a teacher and a seventh-grade student with poor comprehension skills during the first day of reciprocal teaching. The text they are discussing concerns water moccasins.

(1) C: What is found in the southeastern snakes, also the copperhead, rattlesnakes, vipers—they have. I'm not doing this right.
(2) T: All right. Do you want to know about the pit vipers?
(3) C: Yeah.
(4) T: What would be a good question about the pit vipers that starts with the word "why?"
(5) C: (*No response.*)
(6) T: How about, "Why are the snakes called pit vipers?"
(7) C: Why do they want to know that they are called pit vipers?
(8) T: Try it again.
(9) C: Why do they, pit vipers in a pit?
(10) T: How about, "Why do they call the snakes pit vipers?"
(11) C: Why do they call the snakes pit vipers?
(12) T: There you go! Good for you. (Palincsar and Brown, 1984, p. 138)

The mixed success of the child in this example in posing an adequate summarizing question contrasts markedly with his performance on day 15. In that session, the student was to ask a summarizing question about a text on scientists' need to come to the South Pole to study the "southern lights." He responded by saying, "Why do scientists come to the South Pole to study?," to which the teacher responded, "Excellent question! That is what the paragraph is all about" (Palincsar and Brown, 1984, p. 139).

To say that explicit ventriloquation is involved in reciprocal teaching is not to say that some kind of rote learning is being encouraged. If anything, quite the opposite seems to characterize its intent and outcome. In terms of the notion of functional dualism outlined in Chapter 4, reciprocal teaching encourages children to switch from a univocal orientation toward written text to a dialogic orientation. This is a shift toward a much more active interanimation between the voice of the reader and the text than had apparently characterized students' previous approach.

Palincsar and Brown have used the procedure of reciprocal teaching primarily with poor readers. Although its applicability to average or above average readers still awaits detailed examination, the interesting point is that a kind of dialogic contact had apparently not worked for weak readers as it had for average and above average readers. Whereas the latter groups seem to be able to internalize the dialogic structure of the valued forms of reading activity by responding to teachers' utterances (instructional questions), weak readers apparently were not able to do so. In order to achieve a high degree of success with them, a different form of dialogic encounter was required, namely, explicit ventriloquation. In one case, the practice of responding alone seemed to foster the appropriation of the speech genre of instructional questions; in the other, explicit ventriloquation, achieved through reciprocal teaching, was required.

A Summary Overview

If one poses the Bakhtinian question "Who is doing the talking?" in these four illustrations, the answers that emerge are complex and multileveled. In one sense, of course, the individuals producing the utterances are speaking. All one needs to do to be reminded of the individual responsibility assigned to speakers is to witness the response to an utterance deemed incorrect or inappropriate. When the teacher responded to Mikey by saying, "Oh . . . That's not a good answer," her comment was based on the assumption that Mikey was doing the talking.

In a second sense, however, the four illustrations reflect various ways in which voices other than that of the individual producing the concrete utterance can be heard. In some cases, this multivoicedness stems from the utterances of other concrete voices that have been part of the speaker's experience. In the example of reciprocal teaching interaction, an utterance used by the student is appropriated directly from the teacher.

(10) T: How about, "Why do they call the snakes pit vipers?"
(11) C: Why do they call the snakes pit vipers?
(12) T: There you go! Good for you. (Palincsar and Brown, 1984, p. 138)

In such cases there is a clear and direct appropriation of one voice by another. In other cases the multivoicedness that grows out of the interanimation of two specific, concrete voices is less obvious. In the illustration involving noninstructional experience statements, the presence of teachers' voices was manifested in the relative *absence* of certain kinds of referentially semantic content in students' utterances. In this case the tendency to avoid certain areas of referentially semantic content because of previous dialogic encounters produces what Bakhtin termed "the word with a sideward glance" (1984, p. 196).

In contrast to the multivoicedness that grows out of the interanimation of concrete utterances in the "primordial dialogue of discourse," I have focused on how utterances appropriate *types* of voices, specifically, those that appear in the form of speech genres and social languages. By focusing on speech genres as mediational means, one is constantly reminded that mediated action is inextricably linked to historical, cultural, and institutional settings, and that the social origins of individual mental functioning extend beyond the level of intermental functioning. Because utterances inevitably invoke a speech genre, it is no longer possible to view dialogue in terms of two localized voices.

In all four illustrations, the voices being appropriated by the children can be fully interpreted only if one goes beyond the individual speakers involved. In order to interpret what it is that they have said and to identify who it is that is doing the talking one must look to the speech genres appropriated in speakers' utterances. Naturally, the primordial dialogue of discourse provides the concrete mechanism through which one gains access to speech genres, but by invoking the notion of speech genre this dialogue is no longer solely a process occurring between individuals. If one asks why the teachers produced the kinds of questions, directives, and other utterances that provided the socializing context for their students, it is clear that these teachers were also ventriloquating through speech genres characteristic of the sociocultural context.

In identifying the speech genres being appropriated in the teachers' utterances, one might be tempted to say that "the voice of the teacher's manual" or "the voice of the curriculum" can be heard. Indeed, some curriculum materials provide specific utterances to be appropriated by the teacher just as the teacher in the reciprocal teaching example provided specific utterances to be appropriated by the child. Yet an account proceeding only to this point would not be getting to the heart of the matter. To understand why teachers' manuals are written as they are, one must examine the forces at work on a more general cultural, historical, and institutional level.

This is precisely the point at which the need for a sociocultural approach and an interdisciplinary orientation comes most clearly into focus. Attempting to understand mental functioning or mediational means in purely psychological terms is destined, at best, to remain incomplete in an essential way. As an illustration, let us consider two issues that have been widely studied in connection with sociocultural setting. These issues are quite suggestive of how a sociocultural approach might proceed in the future.

The first is the construct of *rationality* as outlined in social theory by Weber (1968, 1978) and extended by theorists such as Habermas (1984). According to Weber, the notion of rationality is a tool for analyzing capitalist economic activity, bourgeois private law, and bureaucratic authority. It emerges in modern technological societies in various spheres of social action (such as the economic and legal spheres, especially as bureaucratically organized), and is associated with the treatment of a wide range of phenomena, including the individual, in terms of abstract categories. In examining the category of economic action, Weber defined "formal" rationality as follows: "A system of economic activity will be called 'formally' rational according to the degree in which the provision for needs, which is essential to every rational economy, is capable of being expressed in numerical, calculable terms, and is so expressed" (1978, p. 85).

One of the ways rationality is manifested in modern technological societies is in the employment and privileging of speech genres, in particular, in the mastery of technocratic (Zinchenko, 1988) and scientific speech genres. The power of these speech genres is clearly revealed in a wide range of adult forms of discourse, such as that concerned with the nuclear arms debate, where a "decontextualized mode of discourse" (Wertsch, 1988) or "technospeak" (Cohn, 1987) is privileged. As we said in the illustration concerning "official science" in the classroom, the mastery of this privileging pattern is well under way even in the first years of formal schooling. Wertsch and Minick (1990) have argued that the development of this pattern is encouraged by teacher and student use of scientific concepts in the discourse of the classroom.

All this is not to say that an account of rationality can be reduced to an analysis of speech genres. But the analysis of speech genres does provide an essential clue in understanding how rationality has come to play such an important role in modern consciousness and how it has come to be so readily accepted as reflecting a "natural" order. It is clearly a construct whose interpretation requires the cooperation of investigators from several disciplinary perspectives.

A second social science issue with obvious implications for an account of the speech genres that shape speaking and thinking is *reproduction*. This notion has been used extensively in social theory, sociology, and anthropology and concerns the tendency for social classes to reproduce themselves. As Pierre Bourdieu (1984) and others have argued, the criteria for membership in various classes may be shifting from economic to "cultural" capital, but the general process of reproduction retains its crucial status.

Bourdieu's analyses and others like them, which rely on cultural interpretation and on statistical trends involving large groups, have produced several major insights into the nature of class structure in modern societies. Of particular importance for an analysis of speech genres and their patterns of privileging are his findings on cultural capital and its reproduction. They suggest that the production and reproduction of cultural capital may serve a major function in shaping the existence of privileging and its patterns. By the same token, an account of speech genres may have a great deal to offer the research efforts of investigators such as Bourdieu because it can provide insight into the concrete practices, specifically in the form of mediated action, that underlie the broad statistical trends identified in sociological research.

Because the sociocultural approach to mediated action I have outlined focuses on speech genres as mediational means, it can enter into fruitful contact with analytic constructs normally considered to be beyond the boundaries of psychology and sociocultural settings other than those I have examined. And it can of course be expanded by taking into consideration many other issues in the social sciences and humanities in addition to rationality and reproduction. The overall goal is to identify agents and units of analysis that do not preclude interdisciplinary discourse.

It is my hope that the ideas I have presented here will do more than simply encourage a more integrated and productive approach to issues in academic discourse. If speech genres provide a crucial link between psychological processes as they currently exist and their cultural, historical, and institutional settings, then they may also reveal important opportunities for positive change. Of course, one cannot produce effective change simply by changing the speech genres involved; the account of mediated action in sociocultural settings I have outlined argues against focusing on any single aspect of the overall picture in isolation. But a capacity to recognize specific speech genres and their patterns of privileging would provide an analytic tool, one that is currently all too infrequently encountered, for understanding sociocultural settings and the psychological processes associated with them. This in turn would allow us to free ourselves from undesirable patterns and create new patterns. There can be no higher goal for scholarship in the social sciences and humanities.

References

Bakhtin, M. M. 1981. *The dialogic imagination: Four essays by M. M. Bakhtin,* ed. Michael Holquist, trans. Caryl Emerson and Michael Holquist. Austin: University of Texas Press.

Bakhtin, M. M. 1984. *Problems of Dostoevsky's poetics,* ed. and trans. Caryl Emerson. Minneapolis: University of Minnesota Press.

Bakhtin, M. M. 1986. *Speech genres and other late essays,* ed. Caryl Emerson and Michael Holquist, trans. V. W. McGee. Austin: University of Texas Press.

Bartlett, F. C. 1935. *Remembering: A study of experimental and social psychology.* Cambridge: Cambridge University Press.

Bateson, Gregory. 1972. *Steps to an ecology of mind: A revolutionary approach to man's understanding of himself.* New York: Ballantine.

Bauman, R., J. T. Irvine, and S. Philips. 1987. Performance, speech community, and genre: A critical review of concepts in the ethnography of speaking. *Working papers and proceedings of the Center for Psychosocial Studies,* no. 11. Chicago: Center for Psychosocial Studies.

Bellah, R. N., R. Madsen, W. M. Sullivan, A. Swidler, and S. M. Tipton. 1985. *Habits of the heart: Individualism and commitment in American life.* Berkeley and Los Angeles: University of California Press.

Bernstein, Basil. 1975. *Class, codes, and control.* Vol. 3. *Toward a theory of educational transmission.* London: Routledge and Kegan Paul.

Berry, J. W. 1985. Cultural psychology and ethnic psychology: A comparative analysis. In *From a different perspective: Studies of behavior across cultures,* ed. I. Reyes and Y. Poortinga. Lisse: Swets and Zeitlinger.

Bivens, J. A., and L. E. Berk. 1990. A longitudinal study of the development of elementary school children's private speech. *Merrill-Palmer quarterly* 36:443–463.

Blonskii, P. P. 1921. *Ocherki po nauchnoi psikhologii* [Essays in scientific psychology]. Moscow: Gosudarstvennoe Izdatel'stvo.

Boas, Franz. 1916. *The mind of primitive man.* New York: Macmillan.

Boas, Franz. 1966. Introduction to *Handbook of American Indian languages*. Lincoln: University of Nebraska Press.

Bourdieu, Pierre. 1984. *Distinction: A social critique of the judgement of taste,* trans. Richard Nice. Cambridge, Mass.: Harvard University Press.

Brown, A. L., and L. A. French. 1978. The zone of proximal development: Implications for intelligence testing in the year 2000. In *Human intelligence: Perspectives on theory and measurement,* ed. R. J. Sternberg and D. K. Detterman. Norwood, N.J.: Ablex.

Brown, A. L., and A. S. Palincsar. 1982. Inducing strategic learning from texts by means of informed, self-control training. *Topics in learning and learning disabilities* 2(1):1–17.

Bruner, Jerome. 1976. Psychology and the image of man. *Times literary supplement,* Dec. 17.

Bruner, Jerome. 1986. *Actual minds, possible worlds*. Cambridge, Mass.: Harvard University Press.

Bruner, Jerome, and D. R. Olson. 1977–78. Symbols and texts as the tools of intellect. *Interchange* 8(4):1–15.

Chafe, W. L. 1974. Language and consciousness. *Language* 50:111–133.

Chafe, W. L. 1976. Givenness, contrastiveness, definiteness, subjects, topics, and point of view. In *Subject and topic,* ed. C. N. Li. New York: Academic Press.

Chomsky, Noam. 1965. *Aspects of the theory of syntax*. Cambridge, Mass.: MIT Press.

Chomsky, Noam. 1966. *Cartesian linguistics: A chapter in the history of rationalist thought*. New York: Harper and Row.

Cicourel, A. V. 1981. Language and medicine. In *Language in the USA,* ed. C. A. Ferguson and S. B. Heath. Cambridge: Cambridge University Press.

Clark, Katerina, and Michael Holquist. 1984. *Mikhail Bakhtin*. Cambridge, Mass.: Harvard University Press.

Cohn, Carol. 1987. Sex and death in the rational world of defense intellectuals. *Signs* 12:687–718.

Cole, Michael. 1985. The zone of proximal development: Where culture and cognition create each other. In *Culture, communication, and cognition: Vygotskian perspectives,* ed. J. V. Wertsch. New York: Cambridge University Press.

Cole, Michael. In press. Cultural psychology: A once and future discipline? In *Nebraska symposium on motivation: Cross-cultural perspectives,* ed. J. J. Berman. Lincoln: vol. 37, University of Nebraska Press.

Cole, Michael, and Sylvia Scribner. 1974. *Culture and thought: A psychological introduction*. New York: Wiley.

Descartes, René. 1908. *Rules for the direction of understanding,* ed. Charles Adams and Paul Tannery. Paris.

Dewey, John. 1901. *Contributions to Education No. 2: Psychology and Social Practice*. Chicago: University of Chicago Press.

Donaldson, Margaret. 1978. *Children's minds*. New York: Norton.

Emerson, Caryl. 1989. Personal communication.

Gal'perin, P. Ya. 1969. Stages in the development of mental acts. In *A handbook of contemporary Soviet psychology,* ed. Michael Cole and Irving Maltzman. New York: Basic Books.

Geertz, Clifford. 1973. *The interpretation of cultures*. New York: Basic Books.

Gilligan, Carol. 1982. *In a different voice: Psychological theory and women's development*. Cambridge, Mass.: Harvard University Press.

Goffman, Erving. 1959. *The presentation of self in everyday life*. Garden City, New York: Doubleday Anchor.

Goffman, Erving. 1976. Replies and responses. *Language in society* 5:257–313.

Goodnow, Jacqueline. 1990. Using sociology to extend psychological accounts of cognitive development. *Human development* 33:81–107.

Goudena, P. P. 1983. *Private speech: An analysis of its social and self-regulatory functions*. Ph.D. diss., State University of Utrecht, The Netherlands.

Goudena, P. P. 1987. The social nature of private speech of preschoolers during problem solving. *International journal of behavioral development* 10:187–206.

Gumperz, J. J. 1983. *Discourse strategies. Studies in interactional sociolinguistics*. New York: Cambridge University Press.

Habermas, Jurgen. 1970. *Toward a rational society: Student protest, science, and politics*. Boston: Beacon Press.

Habermas, Jurgen. 1984. *The theory of communicative action*. Vol. 1. *Reason and the rationalization of society,* trans. T. McCarthy. Boston: Beacon Press.

Haeckel, Ernst. 1874. *The evolution of man: A popular exposition of the principal points of human ontogeny and phylogeny*. New York: International Science Library.

Hagstrom, Fran, and J. V. Wertsch. (in preparation). The role of noninstructional experience statements in classroom discourse.

Hall, G. S. 1906. *Youth, its education, regimen, and hygiene*. New York: D. Appleton.

Harris, Roy. 1981. *The language myth*. London: Duckworth.

Hatano, Giyoo, and Kayoko Inagaki. In press. Sharing cognition through collective comprehension activity. In *Perspectives on socially shared cognition,* ed. L. Resnick. Washington, D.C.: American Psychological Association.

Heath, Shirley Brice. 1983. *Ways with words: Language, life, and work in communities and classrooms*. Cambridge: Cambridge University Press.

Hickmann, Maya. 1985. The implications of discourse skills in Vygotsky's developmental theory. In *Culture, communication, and cognition: Vygot-skian perspectives,* ed. J. V. Wertsch. New York: Cambridge University Press.

Hickmann, Maya, and J. V. Wertsch. 1978. Adult-child discourse in problem solving situations. In *Papers from the fourteenth regional meeting of the Chicago Linguistic Society.* Chicago: Chicago Linguistic Society.

Hoffer, William. 1985. The Dvorak keyboard: Is it your type? *Nation's business* 73 (August, 1985):38–40.

Holquist, Michael. 1981. The politics of representation. In *Allegory in representation: Selected papers from the English Institute,* ed. S. Greenblatt, 163–183. Baltimore: Johns Hopkins University Press.

Holquist, Michael. 1986. Introduction to *Speech genres and other late essays,* by M. M. Bakhtin. Austin: University of Texas Press.

Holquist, Michael, and Caryl Emerson. 1981. Glossary for *The dialogic imagination: Four essays by M. M. Bakhtin,* ed. Michael Holquist. Trans. Michael Holquist and Caryl Emerson. Austin: University of Texas Press.

Hutchins, E. In press. The social organization of distributed cognition. In *Perspectives on socially shared cognition,* ed. L. Resnick. Washington, D.C.: American Psychological Association.

Hymes, Dell. 1966. Two types of linguistic relativity (with examples from Amerindian ethnography). In *Sociolinguistics, Proceedings of the UCLA sociolinguistics conference, 1964,* ed. W. Bright, pp. 114–167. Janua Linguarum, series major, no. 20. The Hague: Mouton.

Ivanov, V. V. 1974. The significance of M. M. Bakhtin's ideas on sign, utterance, and dialogue for modern semiotics. In *Semiotics and structuralism: Readings from the Soviet Union,* ed. H. Baran. White Plains, N.Y.: International Arts and Sciences Press.

Ivanov, V. V. 1976. *Ocherki po istorii semiotiki v SSSR* [*Essays on the history of semiotics in the USSR*]. Moscow: Izdatel'stvo Nauka.

James, William. 1916. *Pragmatism: A new name for some old ways of thinking.* New York: Longmans, Green.

Janet, Pierre. 1926–27. La pensee interieure et ses troubles. Course given at the College de France.

Janet, Pierre. 1928. *De l'angoisse a l'extase: Etudes sur les croyances et les sentiments.* Vol. 2. *Les sentiments fondamentaux.* Paris: Librairie Felix Alcan.

Jarvie, I. C. 1972. *Concepts and society.* London: Routledge and Kegan Paul.

Karmiloff-Smith, Annette. 1979. *A functional approach to child language.* Cambridge: Cambridge University Press.

Kearins, J. M. 1981. Visual spatial memory in Australian Aboriginal children of desert regions. *Cognitive psychology* 13:434–460.

Kearins, J. M. 1986. Visual spatial memory in Aboriginal and white Australian children. *Australian journal of psychology* 38(3):203–214.

Knorr-Cetina, Karin. 1981. *The manufacture of knowledge: An essay on the constructivist and contextualized nature of science.* Oxford: Pergamon Press.

Kohlberg, Lawrence, J. Yaeger, and E. Hjertholm. 1968. Private speech: Four studies and a review of theories. *Child development* 39:691–736.

Köhler, Wolfgang. 1921a. *Intelligenzpruefungen an Menschenaffen* [Intelligence testing of great apes]. Berlin: J. Springer.

Köhler, Wolfgang. 1921b. Zur Psychologie des Schimpansen [On the psychology of chimpanzees]. *Psychologische forschung*, no. 1:2–46.

Köhler, Wolfgang. 1925. *The mentality of apes.* New York: Harcourt, Brace.

Latour, Bruno, and Steve Woolgar. 1986. *Laboratory life: The construction of scientific facts.* Princeton: Princeton University Press.

Lave, Jean. 1988. *Cognition in practice: Mind, mathematics and culture in everyday life.* Cambridge: Cambridge University Press.

LCHC (Laboratory of Comparative Human Cognition, University of California, San Diego). 1983. Culture and cognitive development. In *Mussen's handbook of child psychology,* ed. William Kessen. 4th ed. Vol. 1. New York: Wiley.

Lee, B. 1985. The intellectual origins of Vygotsky's semiotic analysis. In *Culture, communication, and cognition: Vygotskian perspectives,* ed. J. V. Wertsch. New York: Cambridge University Press.

Leont'ev, A. A. 1970. Social and natural in semiotics. In *Biological and social factors in psycholinguistics,* ed. John Morton. Urbana: University of Illinois Press.

Leont'ev, A. N. 1932. Studies on the cultural development of the child. *Journal of genetic psychology* 40:52–83.

Leont'ev, A. N. 1959. *Problemy razvitiya psikhiki.* Moscow: Izdatel'stvo Moskovskogo Universiteta. Published in English as *Problems in the development of mind* (Moscow: Progress Publishers, 1981).

Leont'ev, A. N. 1975. *Deyatel'nost', soznanie, lichnost'.* Leningrad: Izdatel'stvo Politicheskoi Literaturi. Published in English as *Activity, consciousness, personality* (Englewood Cliffs, N.J.: Prentice Hall, 1978).

Leont'ev, A. N. 1981. The problem of activity in psychology. In *The concept of activity in Soviet psychology,* ed. J. V. Wertsch. Armonk, N.Y.: M. E. Sharpe.

Levina, R. E. 1981. L. S. Vygotsky's ideas about the planning function of speech in children. In *The concept of activity in Soviet psychology,* ed. J. V. Wertsch. Armonk, N.Y.: M. E. Sharpe.

Lévy-Bruhl, Lucien. 1910. *Les fonctions mentales dans les societes inferieures.* Paris: F. Alcan.

Lévy-Bruhl, Lucien. 1923. *Primitive mentality,* trans. L. A. Clare. London: Allen and Unwin. Originally published in 1922.

Linell, Per. 1982. *The written language bias in linguistics.* Linkoping, Sweden: Linkoping University Department of Communication Studies in Communication series. Vol. 2.

Linell, Per. 1988. The impact of literacy on the conception of language: The case of linguistics. In *The written word: Studies in literate thought and action,* ed. R. Saljo, 41–58. Berlin: Springer-Verlag.

Locke, John. 1852. *An essay concerning human understanding.* Philadelphia.

Lotman, Yu. M. 1988a. The semiotics of culture and the concept of a text. *Soviet psychology* 26(3):52–58.

Lotman, Yu. M. 1988b. Text within a text. *Soviet psychology* 26(3):32–51.

Lucy, John. 1987. Grammatical categories and cognitive processes: An historical, theoretical, and empirical re-evaluation of the linguistic relativity hypothesis. Ph.D. diss., University of Chicago.

Lucy, John. In press. *Reflexive language: Reported speech and metapragmatics.* New York: Cambridge University Press.

Lucy, John, and J. V. Wertsch. 1987. Vygotsky and Whorf: A comparative analysis: In *Social and functional approaches to language and thought,* ed. Maya Hickmann. Orlando: Academic Press.

Luria, A. R. 1971. Towards the problem of the historical nature of psychological processes. *International journal of psychology* 6(4):259–272.

Luria, A. R. 1973. *The working brain: An introduction to neuropsychology,* trans. Basil Haigh. New York: Basic Books.

Luria, A. R. 1976a. *Cognitive development: Its cultural and social foundations.* Cambridge, Mass.: Harvard University Press.

Luria, A. R. 1976b. *The nature of human conflicts.* New York: Liveright. Originally published in 1932.

Luria, A. R. 1981. *Language and cognition,* ed. J. V. Wertsch. New York: Wiley Intersciences.

Lyons, John. 1977. *Semantics.* Vol. 1. Cambridge: Cambridge University Press.

Lyons, John. 1981. *Language and linguistics: An introduction.* Cambridge: Cambridge University Press.

Marx, Karl. 1959. Theses on Feuerbach. In *Marx and Engels: Basic writings on politics and philosophy,* ed. L. S. Feuer. Garden City, N.Y.: Doubleday.

Mead, G. H. 1934. *Mind, self, and society from the standpoint of a social behaviorist.* Chicago: University of Chicago Press.

Medvedev, P. N. / M. M. Bakhtin. 1978. *The formal method in literary scholarship: A critical introduction to sociological poetics.* Baltimore: Johns Hopkins University Press.

Mehan, Hugh. 1979. *Learning lessons.* Cambridge, Mass.: Harvard University Press.

Mehan, Hugh. 1989. The construction of an LD student: A case study in the politics of representation. In *People in action,* ed. Jean Lave and S. Chaiklin. New York: Cambridge University Press.

Mehan, Hugh. 1990. The school's work of sorting students. In *Talk and social structure,* ed. D. Boden and D. H. Zimmerman. Cambridge: Polity Press.

Michaels, Sarah. 1981. "Sharing time": Children's narrative styles and differential access to literacy. *Language socialization* 10:423–442.

Middleton, David. 1987. Collective memory and remembering: Some issues and approaches. *Quarterly newsletter of the Laboratory of Comparative Human Cognition* 9:2–5.

Minick, N. J. 1985. L. S. Vygotsky and Soviet activity theory: New perspectives on the relationship between mind and society. Ph.D. diss., Northwestern University.

Minick, N. J. 1987. Introduction to *Thinking and speech,* by L. S. Vygotsky. New York: Plenum.

Minick, N. J., E. Forman, and C. A. Stone, eds. In press. *Education and mind: The integration of institutional, social, and developmental processes.* New York: Oxford University Press.

Morson, G. S. 1986. Preface to *Bakhtin: Essays and dialogues on his work,* ed. G. S. Morson. Chicago: University of Chicago Press.

Morson, G. S., and Caryl Emerson. 1989. Introduction to *Rethinking Bakhtin.* Evanston: Northwestern University Press.

Morson, G. S., and Caryl Emerson. In press. *Mikhail Bakhtin: Creation of a prosaics.* Stanford: Stanford University Press.

Ochs, Elinor. 1988. *Culture and language acquisition: Acquiring communicative competence in Western Samoa.* Cambridge: Cambridge University Press.

Olson, David. 1977. From utterance to text: The bias of language in speech and writing. *Harvard educational review* 47:257–281.

Palincsar, A. S. 1987. An apprenticeship approach to the instruction of comprehension skills. Paper presented at symposium, Perspectives on expert learning: An integrative examination of theoretical and empirical issues. American Education Research Association.

Palincsar, A. S., and A. L. Brown. 1984. Reciprocal teaching of comprehension-fostering and comprehension-monitoring activities. *Cognition and instruction* 1(2):117–175.

Palincsar, A. S., and A. L. Brown. 1988. Teaching and practicing thinking skills to promote comprehension in the context of group problem solving. *RASE* 9(1):53–59.

Parkinson, G. H. R. 1977. The translation theory of understanding. In *Communication and understanding,* ed. G. Vesey, 1–19. London: Hassocks.

Philips, Susan U. 1987. The concept genre and the study of language and culture. *Working papers and proceedings of the Center for Psychosocial Studies,* no. 11. Chicago: Center for Psychosocial Studies.

Piaget, Jean. 1923. *Le langage et la pensée chez l'enfant*. Paris. Published in English as *The language and thought of the child* (New York: Harcourt, Brace, 1926). Published in Russian as *Rech' i myshlenie rebenka* (Moscow and Leningrad: Gosizdat, 1932).

Popper, K. R. 1972. *Objective knowledge*. Oxford: Clarendon Press.

Potebnya, A. A. 1913. *Mysl' i yazyk* [Thought and language]. Khar'kov: Tipografiya "Mirnyi Trud."

Price-Williams, Douglas. 1980. Toward the idea of cultural psychology: A superordinate theme for study. *Journal of cross-cultural psychology* 11: 75–89.

Radzikhovskii, L. A. 1979. Osnovnie stadii nauchnogo tvorchesta L. S. Vygotskogo [Fundamental stages in Vygotsky's scientific work]. Diss. (kandidatskaya), Moscow State University.

Radzikhovskii, L. A., ed. 1982. Commentary. *Sobranie sochinenii, Tom vtoroi, Problemy obshchei psikhologii* by L. S. Vygotsky [Collected works, vol. 2: Problems of general psychology]. Moscow: Izdatel'stvo Pedagogika.

Reddy, M. J. 1979. The conduit metaphor: A case of frame conflict in our language about language. In *Metaphor and thought,* ed. A. Ortony. Cambridge: Cambridge University Press.

Rogoff, Barbara. 1990. *Apprenticeship in thinking: Cognitive development in social context*. New York: Oxford University Press.

Rogoff, Barbara, and Jean Lave, eds. 1984. *Everyday cognition: Its development in social contexts*. Cambridge, Mass.: Harvard University Press.

Rogoff, Barbara, and J. V. Wertsch, eds. 1984. Children's learning in the "zone of proximal development." In *New directions for child development,* no. 23. San Francisco: Jossey-Bass.

Rommetveit, R. 1979. Deep structure of sentence versus message structure: Some critical remarks on current paradigms, and suggestions for an alternative approach. In *Studies of language, thought and verbal communication,* ed. R. Rommetveit and R. Blakar. London: Academic Press.

Rommetveit, R. 1988. On literacy and the myth of literal meaning. In *The written word: Studies in literate thought and action,* ed. R. Saljo, 13–40. Berlin: Springer-Verlag.

Rubinshtein, S. L. 1957. *Bytie i soznanie* [Being and consciousness]. Moscow: Izdatel'stvo Akademii Nauk, SSSR.

Rumelhart, D. E., J. L. McClelland, and the PDP Research Group. 1986. *Parallel distributed processing: Explorations in the microstructure of cognition*. Cambridge, Mass.: MIT Press.

Sapir, Edward. 1921. *Language: An introduction to the study of speech*. New York: Harcourt, Brace.

Sapir, Edward. 1931. Conceptual categories in primitive languages. *Science* 74:578.

Sarason, S. B. 1981. An asocial psychology and a misdirected clinical psychology. *American psychologist* 36(8):827–836.

Saussure, Ferdinand de. 1959. *Course in general linguistics*. New York: Philosophical Library.

Schank, R. C., and R. P. Abelson. 1977. *Scripts, plans, goals and understanding: An inquiry into human knowledge structures*. Hillsdale, N.J.: Erlbaum.

Schieffelin, Bambi, and Elinor Ochs. 1986. Language and socialization. In *Annual review of anthropology*, ed. B. Siegel. Palo Alto: Annual Reviews.

Scribner, Sylvia. 1977. Modes of thinking and ways of speaking. In *Thinking: Readings in cognitive science*, ed. P. N. Johnson-Laird and P. C. Wason. New York: Cambridge University Press.

Scribner, Sylvia. 1985. Vygotsky's uses of history. In *Culture, communication, and cognition: Vygotskian perspectives*, ed. J. V. Wertsch. New York: Cambridge University Press.

Scribner, Sylvia, and Michael Cole. 1981. *The psychology of literacy*. Cambridge, Mass.: Harvard University Press.

Seve, L. 1978. *Man in Marxist theory and the psychology of personality*. Sussex: Harvester Press.

Shannon, C. E., and W. Weaver. 1949. *The mathematical theory of communication*. Urbana: University of Illinois Press.

Shchedrovitskii, Georgi. 1981. Presentation at the all-union conference: Vygotsky's scientific creativity and contemporary psychology. Moscow, June 23–25.

Sherzer, J. 1987. A discourse-centered approach to language and culture. *American anthropologist* 89:295–309.

Shif, Zh. I. 1935. Razvitie nauchnykh ponyatii u shkol'nika: Issledovanie k voprosu umstvennogo razvitiya shkol'nika pri obuchenii obshchestvovedeniya [The development of scientific concepts in the school child: The investigation of intellectual development of the school child in social science instruction]. Moscow-Leningrad: Gosudarstvennoe Uchebno-Pedagogicheskoe Izdatel'stvo.

Shotter, J. 1982. The political economy of selfhood: The social psychodynamics of the Cold War. Lecture in the Nottingham Peace Lectures series, University of Nottingham, England.

Shweder, R. A. 1990. Cultural psychology—What is it? In *Cultural psychology: Essays on comparative human development*, ed. J. W. Stigler, R. A. Shweder, and Gilbert Herdt. New York: Cambridge University Press.

Silverstein, M. 1987. Cognitive implications of a referential hierarchy. In *Social and functional approaches to language and thought*, ed. Maya Hickmann. Orlando: Academic Press.

Sinha, Chris. 1989. Evolution, development, and the social production of mind. *Cultural dynamics* 2(2).

Smirnov, A. N. 1975. *Razvitie i sovremennoe sostoyanie psikhologicheskoi nauki v SSSR* [The development and current state of psychology in the USSR]. Moscow: Izdatel'stvo Pedagogika.

Stocking, George. 1968. *Race, culture, and evolution: Essays in the history of anthropology.* New York: The Free Press.

Strawson, P. F. 1971. *Logico-linguistic papers.* London: Methuen.

Taylor, Charles. 1985a. *Human agency and language: Philosophical papers 1.* New York: Cambridge University Press.

Taylor, Charles. 1985b. *Philosophy and the human sciences. Philosophical papers 2.* New York: Cambridge University Press.

Taylor, Charles. 1989. *Sources of the self: The making of modern identity.* Cambridge, Mass.: Harvard University Press.

Tharp, Roland G., and Ronald Gallimore. 1988. *Rousing minds to life: Teaching, learning, and schooling in social context.* New York: Cambridge University Press.

Titunik, I. R. 1986. The Bakhtin problem: Concerning Katerina Clark and Michael Holquist's *Mikhail Bakhtin. Slavic and East European journal* 30(1):91–95.

Titunik, I. R., and N. H. Bruss. 1976. Preface to *Freudianism: A Marxist critique,* by V. N. Voloshinov. New York: Academic Press.

Todorov, Tzvetan. 1984. *Mikhail Bakhtin: The dialogic principle,* trans. Wlad Godzich. Minneapolis: University of Minnesota Press.

Toulmin, Stephen. 1980. Toward reintegration: An agenda for psychology's second century. In *Psychology and society: In search of symbiosis,* ed. R. A. Kasschau and F. S. Kessel. New York: Holt, Rinehart and Winston.

Trevarthen, Colwyn. 1979. Communication and co-operation in early infancy: A description of primary intersubjectivity. *Before speech,* ed. M. Bullowa. Cambridge: Cambridge University Press.

Tulviste, Peeter. 1978. On the origins of theoretic syllogistic reasoning in culture and in the child. In *Problems of communication.* Tartu, USSR: Tartu University Press.

Tulviste, Peeter. 1986. Ob istoricheskoi geterogennosti verbal'nogo myshleniya [The historical heterogeneity of verbal thinking]. In *Myshlenie, obshchenie, praktika: Sbornik nauchnykh trudov* [Thinking, society, practice: A collection of scientific works], ed. Ya. A. Ponomarev, 19–29. Yaroslavl': Yaroslavskii Gosudarstvennyi Pedagogicheskii Institut im. K. D. Ushinskogo.

Tulviste, Peeter. 1987. L. Lévy-Bruhl and problems of the historical development of thought. *Soviet psychology* 25(3):3–21.

Tulviste, Peeter. 1988. *Kul'turno-istoricheskoe razvitie verbal'nogo myshlenie (psikhologicheskie issledovaniya)* [The cultural-historical development of verbal thinking (psychological research)]. Tallin: Valgus.

Uspensky, Boris. 1973. *A poetics of composition: The stucture of the artistic text and typology of a compositional form,* trans. V. Zavarin and S. Wittig. Berkeley and Los Angeles: University of California Press.

Uzgiris, I. C. 1989. Infants in relation: Performers, pupils, and partners. In *Child development today and tomorow,* ed. William Damon, San Francisco: Jossey-Bass.

Van der Veer, R. I., and M. H. van Ijzendoorn. 1985. Vygotsky's theory of the higher psychological processes: Some criticism. *Human development* 28:1–9.

Voloshinov, V. N. 1973. *Marxism and the philosophy of language,* trans. L. Matejka and I. R. Titunik. New York: Seminar Press. Originally published in 1929.

Voloshinov, V. N. 1988. *Freudianism: A critical sketch.* Bloomington: Indiana University Press. Translated by I. R. Titunik and edited in collaboration with N. H. Bruss.

Vygotsky, L. S. 1929. The problem of the cultural development of the child. *Journal of genetic psychology* 36:415–434.

Vygotsky, L. S. 1934a. *Myshlenie i rech': Psikhologicheskie issledovaniya* [Thinking and speech: Psychological investigations]. Moscow and Leningrad: Gosudarstvennoe Sotsial'no Ekonomicheskoe Izdatel'stvo

Vygotsky, L. S. 1934b. Problema obucheniya i umstvennogo razvitiya v shkol'nom vozraste [The problem of instruction, and cognitive development during the school years]. In his *Umstvennoe razvitie detei v protsesse obucheniya* [Cognitive development in children in the process of instruction]. Moscow and Leningrad: Uchpedgiz, 1935.

Vygotsky, L. S. 1956. *Izbrannye psikhologicheskie issledovaniya* [Selected psychological investigations]. Moscow: Izdatel'stvo Akademii Pedagogicheskikh Nauk.

Vygotsky, L. S. 1960. *Razvitie vysshykh psikhicheskikh funktsii* [The development of higher mental functions]. Moscow: Izdatel'stvo Akademii Pedagogicheskikh Nauk.

Vygotsky, L. S. 1972. Problema periodizatsii etapov v detskom vozraste [The problem of stage periodization in child development]. *Voprosy psikhologii* [Problems of psychology] 2:114–123.

Vygotsky, L. S. 1977. Iz tet'ryadei L. S. Vygotskogo [From the notebooks of L. S. Vygotsky]. *Vestnik Moskovskogo Universiteta: Seriya psikhologii* [Moscow University record: Psychology series] 15:89–95.

Vygotsky, L. S. 1978. *Mind in society: The development of higher psychological processes,* ed. Michael Cole, Vera John-Steiner, Sylvia Scribner, and Ellen Souberman. Cambridge, Mass.: Harvard University Press.

Vygotsky, L. S. 1979. Consciousness as a problem in the psychology of behavior. *Soviet psychology* 17(4):3–35.

Vygotsky, L. S. 1981a. The instrumental method in psychology. In *The concept of activity in Soviet psychology,* ed. J. V. Wertsch. Armonk, N.Y.: M. E. Sharpe.

Vygotsky, L. S. 1981b. The genesis of higher mental functions. In *The concept of activity in Soviet psychology,* ed. J. V. Wertsch. Armonk, N.Y.: M. E. Sharpe.

Vygotsky, L. S. 1981c. The development of higher forms of attention in childhood. In *The concept of activity in Soviet psychology,* ed. J. V. Wertsch. Armonk, N.Y.: M. E. Sharpe.

Vygotsky, L. S. 1982a. *Sobranie sochinenii, Tom pervyi: Voprosy teorii i istorii psikhologii* [Collected works, vol. 1: Problems in the theory and history of psychology]. Moscow: Izdatel'stvo Pedagogika.

Vygotsky, L. S. 1982b. *Sobranie sochinenii, Tom vtoroi, Problemy obshchei psikhologii* [Collected works, vol. 2: Problems of general psychology]. Moscow: Izdatel'stvo Pedagogika.

Vygotsky, L. S. 1983a. *Sobranie sochinenii, Tom tretii. Problemy razvitiya psikhiki* [Collected works, vol. 3: Problems in the development of mind]. Moscow: Izdatel'stvo Pedagogika.

Vygotsky, L. S. 1983b. *Sobranie sochinenii, Tom pyati: Osnovy defektologii* [Collected works, vol. 5: Foundations of defectology]. Moscow: Izdatel'stvo Pedagogika.

Vygotsky, L. S. 1984a. *Sobranie sochinenii, Tom chetvertyi: Detskaya psikhilogii* [Collected works, vol. 4: Child psychology]. Moscow: Izdatel'stvo Pedagogika.

Vygotsky, L. S. 1984b. *Sobranie sochinenii, Tom shestoi: Nauchnoe nasledstvo* [Collected works, vol. 6: Scientific legacy]. Moscow: Izdatel'stvo Pedagogika.

Vygotsky, L. S. 1987. *Thinking and speech,* ed. and trans. N. Minick. New York: Plenum. Translation of Vygotsky, 1982b.

Vygotsky, L. S., and A. R. Luria. 1930. *Etyudy po istorii povedeniya: Obez'yana, primitiv, rebenok* [Essays on the development of behavior: Ape, primitive, child]. Moscow and Leningrad: Gosudarstvennoe Izdatel'stvo.

Weber, Max. 1968. *On charisma and institution building: Selected papers,* ed. S. N. Eisenstadt. Chicago: University of Chicago Press.

Weber, Max. 1978. *Economy and society: An outline of interpretive sociology,* ed. G. Roth and C. Wittich. Berkeley: University of California Press.

Werner, Heinz. 1948. *Comparative psychology of mental development.* New York: International Universities Press.

Wertsch, J. V. 1979a. From social interaction to higher psychological processes: A clarification and application of Vygotsky's theory. *Human development* 22(1):1–22.

Wertsch, J. V. 1979b. The regulation of human action and the given-new organization of private speech. In *The development of self-regulation through private speech,* ed. G. Zivin. New York: Wiley.

Wertsch, J. V. 1980. The significance of dialogue in Vygotsky's account of social, egocentric, and inner speech. *Contemporary educational psychology* 5:150–162.

Wertsch, J. V., ed. 1981. *The concept of activity in Soviet psychology.* Armonk, N.Y.: M. E. Sharpe.

Wertsch, J. V., ed. 1985a. *Culture, communication, and cognition: Vygotskian perspectives.* New York: Cambridge University Press.

Wertsch, J. V. 1985b. Introduction to *Culture, communication, and cognition: Vygotskian perspectives.* New York: Cambridge University Press.

Wertsch, J. V. 1985c. *Vygotsky and the social formation of mind.* Cambridge, Mass.: Harvard University Press.

Wertsch, J. V. 1987. Modes of discourse in the nuclear arms debate. *Current research on peace and violence* 10(2–3):102–112.

Wertsch, J. V. 1988. The fragmentation of discourse in the nuclear arms debate. *Multilingua* 7(1–2):11–33.

Wertsch, J. V., and N. J. Minick. 1990. Negotiating sense in the zone of proximal development. In *Promoting cognitive growth over the life span,* ed. M. Schwebel, C. A. Maher, and N. S. Fagley, 71–88. Hillsdale, N.J.: Erlbaum.

Wertsch, J. V., and C. A. Stone. 1985. The concept of internalization in Vygotsky's account of the genesis of higher mental functions. In *Culture, communication, and cognition,* ed. J. V. Wertsch, 162–179. New York: Cambridge University Press.

Wertsch, J. V., and James Youniss. 1987. Contextualizing the investigator: The case of developmental psychology. *Human development* 30:18–31.

Whorf, Benjamin Lee. 1956. *Language, thought, and reality: Selected writings of Benjamin Lee Whorf,* ed. J. B. Carroll. Cambridge, Mass.: MIT Press. Original works written 1927–1941.

Wittgenstein, Ludwig. 1972. *Philosophical investigations,* trans. G. E. M. Anscombe. Oxford: Basil Blackwell and Mott.

Wiser, Marianne. 1988. The differentiation of heat and temperature: History of science and novice-expert shift. In *Ontogeny, phylogeny, and historical development,* ed. S. Strauss. Norwood, N.J.: Ablex.

Wundt, Wilhelm. 1916. *Elements of folk psychology.* London: Allen and Unwin.

Yakubinskii, L. P. 1923. *O dialogicheskoi rechi* [On dialogic speech]. Petrograd: Trudy Foneticheskogo Instituta Prakticheskogo Izucheniya Yazykov.

Zinchenko, V. P. 1985. Vygotsky's ideas about units for the analysis of mind. In *Culture, communication, and cognition: Vygotskian perspectives,* ed. J. V. Wertsch. New York: Cambridge University Press.

Zinchenko, V. P. 1988. Chelovecheskii intellekt i tekhnokraticheskoe myshlenie [Human intellect and technocratic thinking]. *Kommunist* 3 (1319):96–104.

Zinchenko, V. P., and S. D. Smirnov. 1983. *Metodologicheskie voprosy psikhologii* [Methodological problems of psychology]. Moscow: Izdatel'stvo Moskovskogo Universiteta.

Name Index

Bacon, F., 125
Bakhtin, M. M., 12–13, 16, 48–66, 67–68, 69–71, 73–75, 78–86, 103–105, 106–110, 144
Bartlett, F. C., 27
Bateson, G., 14, 33
Bauman, R., 61
Bellah, R. N., 122–123, 124
Berk, L. E., 41
Bernstein, B., 128
Berry, J. W., 7
Bivens, J. A., 41
Boas, F., 16, 43
Bourdieu, P., 111, 115, 146
Brown, A. L., 28, 139–143
Bruner, J., 1–2, 14, 113
Bruss, N. H., 48
Buhler, K., 42
Bush, G., 63–65

Chafe, W. L., 41
Chomsky, N., 8
Cicourel, A. V., 36
Clark, K., 16, 48, 49, 50, 67, 105
Cohn, C., 145
Cole, M., 7, 16, 22, 28, 78, 94, 95, 131, 132

Darwin, C., 20
Descartes, R., 8, 84
Dewey, J., 2–3
Dickens, C., 59
Donaldson, M., 94, 95

Dukakis, M., 64–65
Dvořák, A., 35

Eisenstein, S., 5
Emerson, C., 12, 48, 49, 51, 57, 59
Engels, F., 20

French, L. A., 28

Gallimore, R., 27, 28
Gal'perin, P. Ya., 90
Geertz, C., 14, 24
Gilligan, C., 76–78, 103
Goffman, E., 10, 84
Goodnow, J., 116
Goudena, P. P., 41
Gumperz, J. J., 57

Habermas, J., 9–11, 13, 24, 111, 145
Haeckel, E., 23
Hagstrom, F., 129, 130
Hall, G. S., 23
Harris, R., 71
Hatano, G., 136
Hegel, G. W. F., 16
Hickmann, M., 40, 80, 108, 112
Hjertholm, E., 41
Hoffer, W., 35
Holquist, M., 12, 16, 48, 49, 50, 51, 57, 58, 59, 67, 68, 70, 104, 105
Hutchins, E., 14, 27
Hymes, D., 44

Subject Index